Poetry Explorers 2009

The South & South East

Edited by Mark Richardson & Claire Tupholme

First published in Great Britain in 2010 by

Remus House
Coltsfoot Drive
Peterborough
PE2 9JX
Telephone: 01733 890066
Website: www.youngwriters.co.uk

All Rights Reserved
Book Design by Spencer Hart
© Copyright Contributors 2010
SB ISBN 978-1-84924-846-4

Foreword

At Young Writers our defining aim is to promote an enjoyment of reading and writing amongst children and young adults. By giving aspiring poets the opportunity to see their work in print, their love of the written word as well as confidence in their own abilities has the chance to blossom.

Our latest competition Poetry Explorers was designed to introduce primary school children to the wonders of creative expression. They were given free reign to write on any theme and in any style, thus encouraging them to use and explore a variety of different poetic forms.

We are proud to present the resulting collection of regional anthologies which are an excellent showcase of young writing talent. With such a diverse range of entries received, the selection process was difficult yet very rewarding. From comical rhymes to poignant verses, there is plenty to entertain and inspire within these pages. We hope you agree that this collection bursting with imagination is one to treasure.

Contents

Nina Manukyan (10) 1

Cage Green Primary School, Tonbridge
Kile Simmonds (8) 1
Tegan Page (8) 2
Isobel Jebb (8) 2
Ethan Jones (8) 3
Sophie Lockyer (8) 3
Emily Chivers (8) 3
Kyran Edwards (8) 4
Tamima Ali (8) 4
Laura Franklin (8) 4
Stephanie Silk (8) 5
Katie Pollard (8) 5
Abigail Laura Harrison (8) 5
Lewis James Davies (8) 6
Ellie Baxter (8) 6
Caitlin Derrick (8) 6
Megan Bishop (8) 7
Jessica Leigh Fullman (8) 7
Hobie Attwood (8) 7
Stuart Beech (8) 8
Amy Allison (8) 8
Ali Muhammed Nadeem (8) 8
Katelyn Carson (8) 9
Joshua Aubrey (8) 9
Amy Rockell (8) 9
Finlay Laughton-Zimmerman (8) 10
Millie McCombe (8) 10
Jay Riddall (8) 10
Chloe Lee (9) 11
Billy Styles (8) 11

Combe Bank School, Sevenoaks
Millie Tyler (7) 11
Lauren Stewart (7) 12
Charlotte Watt (7) 12
Frederica Prime (7) 13

Scarlett Elizabeth Heming (7) 13
Bojena Jean Lewis (7) 14
Alice Martin (7) 14
Annabel Fricker (8) 14
Jasmine Silvester (7) 15
Hannah McGowan (7) 15

Eaton Bray Lower School, Dunstable
Jack Hughes (8) 16
Sam Ballad (9) 17
Matthew Lewis (8) 18
Louie Walker (8) 19
Jake Jarrett (8) 20
Sam Scott (8) 21
Rebecca Watkin (8) 22

Haresfield CE Primary School, Stonehouse
Lara Grint (9) 22
Rudi Savage (10) 23
Sophie Ractliffe (8) 23
Jessica Smith (10) 24
Amber Pirie (10) 24
Oliver Crook (9) 25
Georgia Willis (10) 25
Jimmy Willis (7) 26
Joe Hartshorn (10) 26
Esther Mounce (10) 27
Harry Kirby (10) 27
Ellie Card (10) 28

Hurst Primary School, Bexley
Jessica Peart (10) 28
Jordan Bland (10) 29
Hannah Abrahams (10) 30
Courtney Corcoran (10) 30
Grayce Durden (10) 31
Fiona Burgess (10) 31

Finlay Swain (10)	32
Alexa Terry (10)	32
Tania Heckford (10)	33
Stephanie Holland (10)	33
Billy Cotterell (10)	34
Holly Morris (10)	34
Ben Hubbard	35
Niké Bester (10)	35
Emily Sieglar (10)	36
Ryan Traynor (11)	36
Isabelle Mary Penfold (11)	37
Ellie-Mai Ford (9)	37
Jean-Michel Breytenbach (10)	38
Samantha Ford (10)	38
Alice Lydon (10)	39
Ben Murphy (10)	39
Yasmin Badesha (10)	40
Andrew Ruane (10)	40
Victoria Belk (11)	40
Rebecca Farrelly (9)	41
Charlie Bagnall (11)	41
Lucy Harris (9)	41
Charlie Winter (10)	42
Kaylee Heckford (10)	42
Olivia Ellen Leahy (10)	42
Conor Johnson (11)	43
Noémie Joelle Oster (10)	43
Ben Dalton (10)	43
Morgan Connell (9)	44
Kyle Anthony David Brown (9)	44
Maisie Whittley (10)	44
Miranda Parkin (9)	45
Abigail Stack (9)	45
Ezrie Cornford (9)	45
Brooke Connell (9)	46
Jacob Eller (10)	46
Emily Jenson (9)	46
Emily Roffey (9)	47
Joe Williams (9)	47
Ellie May Collinson (10)	47
Emma Harris (9)	48
Tegan Battersby (9)	48
Tom Shea (9)	48

Emily Jenkins (9)	49
Harry Powley (9)	49
Savannah Golesworthy (9)	49
Georgia Henry	50
Ellie Owen (9)	50
Eliane Newitt (9)	50
Dylan Burke Taber (9)	51
Lauren Couldwell (9)	51
Isaac Sam Mitchell (9)	51
Taylor Whittley (10)	52

Killigrew Primary & Nursery School, St Albans

Holly Olivia Hodgson (10)	52
Jack Mackey (10)	53
Laura Payton (10)	54
Isabel Craven (10)	54
Natasha Wai Ling Chen (11)	55
Philippa Jane Boxford (10)	55
Eleanor Webster (10)	56
Bethany Connor (10)	56
Chantelle Lilly Shaw (10)	57
Alistair Wyllie (10)	57
Gabi Zöe Taylor (10)	58
Harry James Charles Reeves (11)	58
Sam Lachau (10)	59
Ronan Thomas Harris (10)	59
Beatrix Julia Adelina Bramwell (10)	60
Oliver Wells (10)	60
Jessica Jabbitt (10)	61
Luke Aldridge (10)	61
Eleanor Friend (10)	62
Emily Smith (10)	62
Daniel Salter (10)	62
Josephine Ashenhurst (10)	63
Eleanor Wright (10)	63
Chloe Cocks (10)	63
Megan Karen Ann Goalen (10)	64
Rebecca Carter (11)	64
Emma Joy Leto (10)	64

Mandeville Primary School, St Albans

Nour Chaouaytarav (10)	65

Lascell Isaac Maher (10)	65
Najiyah Ali (10)	66
Harry Henderson (11)	66
Nahida Chowdhury (10)	67
Keely Jayne Hardman (10)	67
Charlotte O'Connell (10)	68
Fariha Qureshi (10)	68
Saiyara Choudhury (10)	69
Louis Hollands (11)	69
Ihsan Zaman (10)	70

Mortimer St Mary's School, Reading

Emilia Smith (10)	70
Sophie James (10)	71
Helen Fraser (10)	72
Jenny Foy (10)	72
Toby Payne (10)	73
Emily Scott (10)	73
Linzi Asher (10)	74
Zhanaye Fenty (10)	74
Jake Sainsbury (10)	75
James Bridgland (10)	75
Aqsa Aziz (10)	76
Louisa Collins (10)	76
Joe Margetts (10)	77
Christopher Harris (10)	77
Ryan Riddle (11)	78
William Bray (10)	78
Stephen Gomm (11)	78
Emily Lowe (11)	79
Lauren Jury (10)	79
Chloe O'Rourke (10)	79
Anna Hewison (10)	80
Hamish Patterson (10)	80
Abigail Cottingham (10)	80
Emily Pickett (10)	81
Bethany Vinton (10)	81
Grace Sophia Rose Hewitt (10)	81
Liberty Cairns (10)	82
Laura Munson (10)	82
Jake McKerron (10)	82
Charlotte Masters (10)	83
Charley Tuttle (10)	83
Amanda Brice (11)	83
Tom Holmes (10)	84
Archie Craissati (10)	84
Shea Field (10)	84
Molly Palmer (10)	85
Thomas Adye (10)	85
Isobel Bunt (10)	85
Rachel Thurley (10)	86
Charlie Holmes (10)	86
Georgia Batty (11)	86
Bethan Douglas (10)	87
William Barclay Clark (10)	87
Edward Port (10)	87
Alastair Lavery (11)	88
Joshua Titcombe (10)	88
Tia-Louise Bartlett (10)	88

Ninfield CE Primary School, Ninfield

Mikey Squire (9)	89
Ellen Sheppard (9)	90
Joe Creasey (9)	91

Queen Anne Royal Free CE First School, Windsor

Christopher Shankland (8)	91
Louis Gregory	92
Toby Loughran (8)	92
Premleen Kaur Virdi (8)	93

St David's Primary School, Moreton-in-Marsh

Luke Russell (10)	93
Charlotte Grace Davis (9)	94
Phoebe Peters (10)	95
Lidie Considine (10)	96
Josh Lewis (9)	97
Natasha Hanks (9)	98
Rachel Silcock (10)	99
Connor Moore (11)	100
Colby Townley (10)	101
Charmian Monroe (9)	102
Katie Griffin (9)	103
Thomas Shurmer (10)	103

Amelia Jasinski (9) 104
Henry Oughton (10) 104
Thomas Chapman (10) 105
Monaswee Millward-Brookes (9) 105
Sophie Gould (10) 106
William Wall (10) 107

St Mary's CE Primary School, Welham Green

Callie Parker (8) 108
Bryony Richardson (9) 108
Hannah Yvonne Newell (10) 109
Dana Connell (8) 109
Connor MacKintosh (10) 110
Montana Sutton (9) 110
Megan Ann-Marie Davies (9) 111
Darcie Richardson (9) 111
Jessica Bliss (10) 111
Danielle Tibbitts (9) 112
Matthew Swift (9) 112
Elle-May Axford (10) 112
Amy Louise Settle (9) 113
Megan Waller (9) 113
Caitlin Horne (8) 114

St Mary the Virgin CE Primary School, Hartfield

Ross Dyer (10) 114
Lenny Munn (9) 114
Amelia McElligott (10) 115
Cameron Follows (10) 116
Mollie Kent (10) 117
Lauren Millie Oliver (11) 118
Elizabeth Anne Townsend (10) 119
Amelia Rose Cranham (9) 119
Maia Wellbelove (10) 120
Megan Maria Maunsell (10) 120
Marcus Goldsmith (10) 121
Peter Ottman (10) 121
Kia Ivars (8) 122
Laura Johnson (9) 122
Katelyn Sleet (10) 123
Robert Matthew Howey (10) 123

Zeke Jenkins (10) 124
Kirstie Sherry (10) 124
Maddie Noddings (10) 125
Sam Rickets (10) 125
Alice Willemina Moore (10) 126

St Pancras Catholic Primary School, Lewes

Ben Lyons (9) 126
Rosie Hastings (8) 127
Jodie Watson (9) 127
Rhiannon Davies (9) 127
Oliver Willett (8) 128
Chelsea King (9) 128

Sapperton CE Primary School, Cirencester

Henry Elsey (10) 128
Ismé Mason (9) 129
Erin Grady (11) 129
Ewan Crowden (10) 129

Someries Junior School, Luton

Chloe Mullen (9) 130
Kailan Derrick Pare (9) 131
Inayah Inam (9) 131
Andrew Hughes (9) 132
Paige Wykes (9) 132
Morgan Ella Lougher (9) 133
Natasha Bonner (9) 133
Lauren Dilley (9) 134
Sarah Rigby (9) 134
Ethan Paul Cox (9) 135
Jake Simpkins (9) 135
Leah Irvine (10) 136
Zack Boutwood (9) 136
Luke Cresswell (9) 137
Louie Teakle (9) 137
Benjamin Morrison (9) 138
Oliver Gazeley (9) 138
Kimberley Piper (10) 139
Olivia Victoria Pearce (9) 139
Evie Watts (9) 140

Jack Parrott (9) 140	Abdul Mueez Raja (10) 157
Ben Pennifold (9) 140	Wahab Mahmood (10) 157
Paige Martin (9) 141	Shoaib Ahmed (10) 158
Emilio Vaughan Fletcher (9) 141	Sara Sarfraz (10) 158
Adam Murgatroyd (9) 141	Naadia Ajmal (10) 159
Johnathon Martin (9) 142	Jaskirit Bhandal (10) 159
Jack Rawlings (9) 142	

Tanners Brook Junior School, Southampton

Rajdeep Kaur Chungh (10) 142
Faye Draper (10) 143
Nikita Adams (8) 143
Taylor Robyn Murphy (9) 144
Daniel Hallett (8) 144
Eleanor Thomson (9) 144
Mia Hulland-Banks (8) 145
Emily Holmes (9) 145
Laila Savage (8) 145
Shanice Christians (8) 146

Wexham Court Primary School, Slough

Amanda Cooze (11) 146
Ahmad Abu Mahfouz (11) 147
Samantha Kae Sedano Sotero (10) ... 147
Bilal Ur-Rehman (10) 148
Sidra Chaudhry (10) 148
Manraj Singh Tack (10) 149
Rimsha Asad Satti (11) 149
Tawkir Kamali (10) 150
Bethany Money (10) 150
Amrita Singh (10) 151
Rameez Rashid (10) 151
Kajol Jhandey (10) 152
Kiran Dhuga (10) 152
Sabrina Rukshar Mughal (11) 153
Husna Ahmed (10) 153
Cerys Hanson (10) 154
Alina Parveen Malik (10) 154
Georgina Cooper (10) 155
Damayanti Chatterjee (10) 155
Tiggy Morten (10) 156
Luxana Rasiah (11) 156

The Poems

Poetry Explorers 2009 - The South & South East

The Sea

Oh sea, sea, beautiful sea,
Blue waves, calm wind blowing over me.
The sun is shining, that reflects on the sea
People enjoying themselves under palm trees.
Oh sea, sea, beautiful sea,
How much strength have you got in your feet?
Your clear blue waves glide smoothly on the sand
Like a cute little baby in her mummy's hands.
Oh sea, sea, beautiful sea,
Sometimes you can be dangerous like a bumblebee.
Oh sea, sea, you are sacred to me,
Oh sea, sea, I love you, can't you see?

Nina Manukyan (10)

Happiness

What colour is happiness?
Happiness is the colour of the glimmering Liverpool football kit.

What smell is happiness?
Happiness is the smell of spaghetti Bolognese cooking in the oven.

What taste is happiness?
Happiness is the taste of spaghetti Bolognese
and I love slurping it up.

What feel is happiness?
Happiness is the feel of my big dog snuggling up to me.

What sound is happiness?
Happiness is the sound of a guitar playing really loud
because it makes me laugh.

Kile Simmonds (8)
Cage Green Primary School, Tonbridge

Happiness

What colour is happiness?
Yellow, it reminds me not to look at the sun.

Happiness is . . .
Roses, because they remind me of my great nanny's name.

Happiness is . . .
Lovely chocolate fingers, they are lovely and chocolatey.

Happiness is . . .
It feels like a warm bath and it is lovely and snugly.

Happiness is . . .
It sounds like the wind rustling, it is very cold too.

Tegan Page (8)
Cage Green Primary School, Tonbridge

Happiness

What is happiness?
Happiness is red like roses.
What does it smell like?
It smells like a newborn baby.
What does it taste like?
My dad's curry.
What does it feel like?
Like the feeling of a newborn chick.
What does it sound like?
It sounds like the sea rustling the pebbles.

Isobel Jebb (8)
Cage Green Primary School, Tonbridge

Happiness

What colour is happiness?
Blue, the colour of my football kit.
What does it smell like?
It smells like brand new clothes.
What does it taste like?
It tastes like smoked bacon.
What does it sound like?
A blackbird singing.
What does it feel like?
It feels like a newborn fluffy kitten.

Ethan Jones (8)
Cage Green Primary School, Tonbridge

Unhappiness

Unhappiness is black like a dustbin bag left on its own.
Unhappiness smells like mouldy milk in your fridge.
Unhappiness sounds like thunder at night.
Unhappiness looks like people arguing in the playground.
Unhappiness tastes like out of date lemon cake
sitting in your cupboard.
Unhappiness feels like being lonely in a dark room.
Unhappiness reminds me of people shouting at each other.

Sophie Lockyer (8)
Cage Green Primary School, Tonbridge

Sadness

Sadness is blue like bullying.
Sadness smells like wet tears dripping.
Sadness sounds like waves on the beach.
Sadness tastes like rotten eggs.
Sadness feels like I'm worried.
Sadness reminds me of my great nanny.

Emily Chivers (8)
Cage Green Primary School, Tonbridge

Jealous

Jealous is the colour of bright green grass.
Jealous smells of when someone's eating a Subway
when you're not allowed.
Jealous sounds like when someone is telling secrets about you.
Jealous looks like that Kyran has a PSP and Harry doesn't.
Jealous tastes like you are getting postponed.
Jealous feels like you are getting ice-cold.
Jealous reminds me of friends playing without me.

Kyran Edwards (8)
Cage Green Primary School, Tonbridge

All About Love

Love smells of a Christmas dinner cooking in the oven.
Love sounds like my mum reading to me at night-time
before I go to bed.
Love looks like a hug, warm and comfortable,
Love tastes like a chocolate piece of cake,
which is coming straight out the oven
Love feels like someone kissing you before you leave their house.
Love reminds me of my brother, hugging and playing with me.

Tamima Ali (8)
Cage Green Primary School, Tonbridge

Shyness

Shyness is the colour of blue, like tears.
Shyness smells of sweaty skin.
Shyness sounds like a very small voice.
Shyness looks like somebody shaking.
Shyness tastes like squidgy tomatoes.
Shyness feels like fizzy drink.
Shyness reminds me of standing on a stage
In front of lots of people.

Laura Franklin (8)
Cage Green Primary School, Tonbridge

Delighted

Delighted is yellow like yummy bananas.
Delighted smells like flowers swaying in the breeze.
Delighted sounds like dogs happily barking.
Delighted looks like daffodils as still as a statue.
Delighted tastes like delicious chocolate cake.
Delighted feels like a feather touching your face.
Delighted reminds me of Auntie's guinea pig.

Stephanie Silk (8)
Cage Green Primary School, Tonbridge

Loneliness

Loneliness is grey like rain clouds
Loneliness smells of the sea
Loneliness sounds like doing a test
Loneliness looks like space
Loneliness tastes like water
Loneliness feels like silk
Loneliness reminds me of breaking up with my friends.

Katie Pollard (8)
Cage Green Primary School, Tonbridge

Embarrassed

Embarrassed is red like rosy cheeks.
Embarrassed smells like talcum powder.
Embarrassed sounds like laughter.
Embarrassed looks like crying.
Embarrassed tastes like seawater.
Embarrassed feels like frogspawn.
Embarrassed reminds me of slides.

Abigail Laura Harrison (8)
Cage Green Primary School, Tonbridge

Terrified

Terrified, as black as shadows in your mind.
Terrified is the smell of smoke making you cough.
Terrified as the sound of whistling in the night.
Terrified looks like scary people.
Terrified feels like a boulder crushing you.
Terrified reminds me of gangsters.
Terrified tastes like something lumpy.

Lewis James Davies (8)
Cage Green Primary School, Tonbridge

Cheerful

Cheerful, like my golden bracelet.
Cheerful is the smell of a cake in the oven.
Cheerful is the sound of people talking in the street.
Cheerful is like buttercups in the garden.
Cheerful is the taste of a McDonald's ice cream.
Cheerful is like love in the air.
Cheerful reminds me of my best friends.

Ellie Baxter (8)
Cage Green Primary School, Tonbridge

Abandoned

Abandoned is darkest clouds in the sky when the afternoon comes.
Abandoned smells like lonely chips waiting to be eaten.
Abandoned is the sound of straw rustling in the wind.
Abandoned is seeing people play with their friends outside.
Abandoned is the taste of carrots and broccoli.
Abandoned feels like you're missing out on good things.
Abandoned reminds me of being alone.

Caitlin Derrick (8)
Cage Green Primary School, Tonbridge

Envious

Black is the colour of envious, like a scary hut.
Envious smells like gold.
Envious sounds like a rustle of rare chains.
Envious looks like shimmering beads.
Envious tastes like sausage wrapped in melted cheese.
Envious feels like I need it.
Envious reminds me of selfish.

Megan Bishop (8)
Cage Green Primary School, Tonbridge

Sorrow

Sorrow is grey like clouds.
Sorrow smells like rain scattering down.
Sorrow sounds like waves crashing on the beach.
Sorrow tastes like soft roast potatoes.
Sorrow reminds me of my friends.
Sorrow looks like snow falling.
Sorrow feels like tears dropping.

Jessica Leigh Fullman (8)
Cage Green Primary School, Tonbridge

Anger

Anger is the colour of fire.
Anger is the smell of thick black smoke.
Anger sounds like someone shouting.
Anger looks like lightning.
Anger tastes like red-hot chillies.
Angry feels like someone shouting at me.
Anger reminds me of war.

Hobie Attwood (8)
Cage Green Primary School, Tonbridge

Happiness

Happiness is yellow because of the lovely warm midday sun.
It smells like hot lasagne cooking quickly in the oven.
It tastes like a gigantic meal in the oriental buffet
on a Sunday night.
It feels like the smooth skin of the human body
when my mum gives me a hug.
It sounds like a beautiful tune played by a person on the harp.

Stuart Beech (8)
Cage Green Primary School, Tonbridge

Pleased

Pleased is like sun shining on me,
Flowers blooming in the sky,
Butterflies flapping their sparkling wings.
Pleased is like my mum hugging me.
Pleased is like a rabbit nibbling.
Pleased is like love in the air.
Pleased feels like my family.

Amy Allison (8)
Cage Green Primary School, Tonbridge

Merriness

Merriness is blue like the sky.
Merriness smells like delicious food in the restaurant.
Merriness is the sound of when you have won something,
everyone's clapping.
Merriness feels like me cuddling my dad.
Merriness reminds me of my best friends at school.

Ali Muhammed Nadeem (8)
Cage Green Primary School, Tonbridge

Happiness

Happiness is purple like a lovely flower in the sun.
Happiness smells like spaghetti on the cooker.
Happiness tastes like fish and chips just arrived from the shops.
Happiness feels like a baby just been born.
Happiness sounds like the waves crashing up against the rocks at the seaside.

Katelyn Carson (8)
Cage Green Primary School, Tonbridge

Happiness

As yellow as the sun on a summer's day.
Smells like an unwrapped plastic toy.
Tastes like delicious warm chocolate chip cookies.
I like to hear the splash of enormous curling waves
hitting the beach.
I like to touch jelly, all wibbly-wobbly, cold on a plate, shivering.

Joshua Aubrey (8)
Cage Green Primary School, Tonbridge

Annoyed

Annoyed feels like a horrible feeling
Annoyed looks like an angry face
Annoyed smells like bad eggs
Annoyed tastes like lemon juice
Annoyed sounds like horrible anger.

Amy Rockell (8)
Cage Green Primary School, Tonbridge

Happiness

Happiness is like Liverpool's blazing red top.
It smells like yellow, spicy, hot popcorn chicken from KFC.
It tastes like cold, pink strawberry ice cream in the freezer.
Happiness is like England winning the Cup Final 3-0.
It sounds like fireworks exploding in the dark, beautiful sky.

Finlay Laughton-Zimmerman (8)
Cage Green Primary School, Tonbridge

Happiness

Happiness is blue like the blue cloudless sky.
Happiness smells like new, juicy, fresh strawberries.
Happiness tastes like a delicious roast dinner.
Happiness sounds like people screaming on a roller coaster.
Happiness feels like a fluffy pillow.

Millie McCombe (8)
Cage Green Primary School, Tonbridge

Happiness

It's yellow like a freshly grown rose
It smells like purple lavender growing in the fields.
It reminds me of my mum cooking shepherd's pie.
It feels all bumpy like my bearded dragon's skin.
It sounds like my friend playing a drum and tapping out a beat.

Jay Riddall (8)
Cage Green Primary School, Tonbridge

Happiness

Yellow like the sun shining beautifully.
It smells like sausage and chips cooking in the oven.
It smells yummy.
A packet of beautiful smoky bacon crisps.
It feels like a cover that has just come out of the wash.

Chloe Lee (9)
Cage Green Primary School, Tonbridge

Happy, As Blue As The Sky

Happy, as yellow as the sun.
Happy, as red as a sunset.
Happy, as black as the night-time.
Happy, as white as the clouds.

Billy Styles (8)
Cage Green Primary School, Tonbridge

Silver

Silver is the colour of the stars
Silver is the colour of Mars.
Silver is the colour of an ice sleigh
Silver is the colour of the dew in May
Silver is the colour of metal
Silver is the colour of a kettle.

Millie Tyler (7)
Combe Bank School, Sevenoaks

Why?

Why does the wind blow?
Why is a snail so slow?
Why is a grain of sand so small
And why are the waves so tall?
Why is the sea blue?
Why does an ant have so much to do?
Why do the stars glow?
Why does the river flow?
Why does a baby sleep in a cot?
Why does jam come in a pot?
Why does a dog bark?
Why is the night so dark?

Lauren Stewart (7)
Combe Bank School, Sevenoaks

Question Poem

Who made the trees?
Who made the bees?
Who made the day so bright?
Who made the starry night?
Who made the flowers?
Who made the showers?
Why do dogs bark?
Why do bats like the dark?
Why do the stars shine?
Why do poems rhyme?

Charlotte Watt (7)
Combe Bank School, Sevenoaks

Questions

Who made the first tree?
Who made me?
Who made the dark?
Who made the dogs bark?
Who made the trees so tall?
Who made me so small?
Who made pigs so pink?
Why do we wink?
Why do some boats row?
And who made the stars glow?

Frederica Prime (7)
Combe Bank School, Sevenoaks

Who?

Who made the first tree?
Who made the first bee?
Who made the mermaids sing?
Who made the mermaid's ring?
Who made the cats
Who made the hats?
Who made the dragons soar?
Who made the dragons roar?
Who made the bells ring?
Who made the bells ding?

Scarlett Elizabeth Heming (7)
Combe Bank School, Sevenoaks

Imagine

Imagine a snake as thin as a rake
Imagine a pig wearing a wig
Imagine a dog chopping a log
Imagine a flea having a cup of tea
Imagine a bear sitting on a chair
Imagine a cat wearing a plait
Imagine a giraffe wearing a scarf
Imagine a seal as long as an eel!

Bojena Jean Lewis (7)
Combe Bank School, Sevenoaks

Silver

Silver is the colour of raindrops left behind
Or the colour of dew you might find
Silver is the colour of the moon in the evening
Or the colour of tears streaming.
Silver is the colour of the stars gleaming.
Silver is the colour of a lady's ring.

Alice Martin (7)
Combe Bank School, Sevenoaks

Blue

Blue is the colour of a swimming pool sparkling in the sun
Blue is the colour of a dolphin having lots of fun
Blue is the colour of blueberry pie
Blue is the colour of the bright blue sky
Blue is the colour of the deep blue sea
Blue is the colour for you and me.

Annabel Fricker (8)
Combe Bank School, Sevenoaks

Questions

Who made the cats?
Why are mice so small?
Who made the rats?
And why are trees so tall?
Who made cats purr?
Why are pets so tame?
Who made the bears' fur?
And what is your name?
Who made the cars?
Why do animals leave their mothers so soon?
Who made chocolate bars?
Who made the sun and the moon?
Who made the birds sing?
Who made everything?

Jasmine Silvester (7)
Combe Bank School, Sevenoaks

Brown

Brown is the colour of Marmite dribbled over toast
Brown is the colour of Sunday roast
Brown is the colour of the trunk of a tree
Brown is the colour of a cat you might see
Brown is the colour of a dog
Brown is the colour of a hog
Brown is the colour of people's hair
Brown is the colour of a bear.

Hannah McGowan (7)
Combe Bank School, Sevenoaks

The Magic Box
(Based on 'Magic Box' by Kit Wright)

I will put in my box . . .
A penguin with the most pointed beak
The Eiffel Tower with the spikiest point
And a lizard with the softest skin
A swordfish with the sharpest nose.

I will put in my box . . .
The biggest drum with the largest sound
People singing then a scream.

I will put in my box . . .
My favourite food
Like the biggest tuna sandwich
And the juiciest fruit in the land.

I will put in my box . . .
The best smell of roses ever and apple pie
My box is made of sparkling silk in the corners
And soothing water for a lid
For the sides I will use tusks from an elephant
And tiger skin for the bottom

My box has a lock from a gold cage
Made from bamboos that pandas eat
It has stickers of guitars and pictures of my best holidays.

In my box I will explore the jungle
And swing through the trees like a monkey.

Jack Hughes (8)
Eaton Bray Lower School, Dunstable

The Magic Box
(Based on 'Magic Box' by Kit Wright)

I would put into my box . . .
A picture of my little sister
And one of my favourite films.
The tastes of the fizziest lemonade
And the world's biggest pizza.

I would put in my box . . .
The freshest tuna sandwich
And the hardest maths sums,
The exciting PlayStation game
And the best tasting chocolate.

I would put in my box . . .
A terrific television,
That gives you refreshments
And the delicious smell of fish and chips.

My box is fashioned from:
Gold and silver and a lock of sparkling diamonds.
In the corners are the sourest fruits.

I would relax in my box
Playing on my PlayStation,
Munching my favourite chocolate.

Sam Ballad (9)
Eaton Bray Lower School, Dunstable

The Magic Box
(Based on 'Magic Box' by Kit Wright)

I will put in my box . . .

The red sky and then the black,
Colourful leaves of trees in the autumn,
And the mysterious wail of a werewolf.

I will put in my box . . .

The twinkling of a piano,
The delicious taste of Bourneville chocolate,
And the taste of Texas BBQ pizza.

I will put in my box . . .

The mattress of my comfiest bed,
My teddy I've had since birth,
And the green of a fresh new apple.

My box is fashioned from . . .

The strongest steel,
Ice as cold as the Atlantic Ocean,
And it has small rugby pitches in every corner.

I shall play rugby in my box and relax with Bourneville chocolate in front of my TV tonight

Matthew Lewis (8)
Eaton Bray Lower School, Dunstable

The Magic Box
(Based on 'Magic Box' by Kit Wright)

I will put in my box . . .
A picture of my mum and dad
The sound of the ocean

I will put in my box . . .
A twittering bird
And the sight of dolphins swimming.

I will put in my box . . .
The taste of lovely hot days
And delicious creamy chocolate.

I will put in my box . . .
The smell of cooking bacon
And tomato soup.

I will put in my box . . .
A round football
And some sizzling sausages.

My box is made out of tiger fur,
Shiny crystals and fluffy clouds.

Louie Walker (8)
Eaton Bray Lower School, Dunstable

The Magic Box
(Based on 'Magic Box' by Kit Wright)

I will put in my box . . .
The first goal from Man U
The furriest fluff of all time
The sweet taste of pasta

I will put into the box . . .
A dolphin swimming in the salty sea
The sound of a Maclaren starting up
A million pounds worth of games.

I will put into my box . . .
The fluffiest candyfloss
A chip of gold
And a penguin covered yellow

My box is fashioned with gold and sprinkles of sand in the corners
It is wood that is impossible to break.

I will surf in my box with my friends on the hottest beach on Earth
And go to a restaurant in Germany with my friends.

Jake Jarrett (8)
Eaton Bray Lower School, Dunstable

The Magic Box
(Based on 'Magic Box' by Kit Wright)

I will put in my box . . .
A shiny new video
The very first tooth I had
The music of Michael Jackson

I will put in my box . . .
A disco ball and play it in my box
The sweetest ham on a slice of bread
The best bit of chocolate in the whole world.

I will put in my box . . .
The smell of perfume fluttering around my nose.
The smell of my bedroom, which is beautiful
The touch of play dough, as soft as a cloud in the sky.
The gel is as hard as a solid rock

There are footballs all over the sides of my box
In the middle I will lock away my secrets.
I will survive the seven seas.

Sam Scott (8)
Eaton Bray Lower School, Dunstable

The Magic Box
(Based on 'Magic Box' by Kit Wright)

In my box I will put . . .
A lovely, shiny, silver seashell
On the sparkly golden sand
The taste of delicious chocolate ice cream as cold as ice

In my box I will put . . .
A shiny, silver, see-through stone on the thick golden sand.
The taste of delicious chocolate
The smell of fresh flowers from the sea.

In my magic box I will put . . .
A lovely shiny silver carrot from the muddy field

My box will be made out of diamonds and sea fish.
The key is a sunflower.

Rebecca Watkin (8)
Eaton Bray Lower School, Dunstable

Roses, Trees And A Field Of Green Leaves

Rose the song in the sweet morning dew,
Rose as a melody, a summer bird,
Rose as a sea full of future, a future delight,
Rose as a field of bright green grass,
Rose as a bush, a bush in the sun,
Trees as a clear blue sky,
Trees as a song, sweet grass in a trance,
Trees as a bird high on a mountain,
Trees in a forest, a forest of green,
Trees in a field of dewy grass,
Field as a rainbow of sea-green,
Field as a hand clasping one another,
Field as a child waiting to play,
Field as a field not far from the bay.

Lara Grint (9)
Haresfield CE Primary School, Stonehouse

Monsters Everywhere

Monsters everywhere hiding, creeping
Chasing, sneaking and the places you least expect.
In your head, in the toilet, in your bed,
In the chimney near the street
In the dark corner
Where all the monsters meet
Beware monsters everywhere.

Some you can't even see.
In your flowerpot
In your tree, in your pencil case.
In the library, on a stool, creeping slowly, slowly,
Here and there,
Beware they are everywhere.

They might be eating, they might be sleeping,
They might be big,
They might be small,
They might be no bigger than a stool
Beware, look everywhere!

Rudi Savage (10)
Haresfield CE Primary School, Stonehouse

Pigs

Pigs are fat
Boing-boing
Pigs are noisy
Oink-oink!
Pigs are smelly
Phew
Pigs are pink
That's nice
Pigs are bacon
Yum-yum.

Sophie Ractliffe (8)
Haresfield CE Primary School, Stonehouse

Leaves On The Garden

L eaves on the grass
E ven on the path
A lways changing colour
V ines on leaves
E ven on the trees
S pread all around

O n the window sill
N one on the house

T hey are on the roof
H ills of leaves
E verywhere I go

G rass is covered with leaves
A ll around not a sight of grass
R ound, star shaped, loads of shapes
D own the garden
E very time I wake to see
N ight I see them or day I see them.

Jessica Smith (10)
Haresfield CE Primary School, Stonehouse

Monkeys

Sometimes I wonder
What a monkey can do
Maybe it goes under trees or maybe dreams
Sometimes I wonder what a monkey can do
Can it go to the loo?
Sometimes I wonder what a monkey can do.
But I just found out they live in a zoo!

Amber Pirie (10)
Haresfield CE Primary School, Stonehouse

Worm's Eye-View Of Earth

Thud! Thud! Ow! Here comes the charging cow
Up above enemies galore
You are not safe on the seashore
Ah peace at last, no, studs coming in fast
Let's go bye-bye
What's that huh? A bird's eye
Oh now I will die
Here comes the bird, grab and then fly away
Till another day
Oh look, time to go
Just wriggle with the flow
Yeah, tree to Earth *drop-drop*
Belly flop
Splish-splash, massive crash
Flip-flop, drip-drop
This is how you see.
The worm's eye-view, so chuckle with glee.

Oliver Crook (9)
Haresfield CE Primary School, Stonehouse

First Day

Today is my first day at school, wondering if this will be a bore.
Our car is going round a bend, hoping I will see my friends.
We arrive at my school, it looks quite cool.
My class is very colourful, this is really wonderful.
I look around, this is quite safe and sound.
Wait, in come some boys, they're making a lot of noise.
Time for dinner, I'm a winner.
I sit by my friend Millie, she can be quite silly.
I play with a skipping rope, lessons are soon I hope.
Time for my last lesson, I ask a lot of questions
Home time, I get in the line
Today was my first day at school, it was cool!

Georgia Willis (10)
Haresfield CE Primary School, Stonehouse

15 Things You Can Do In Town To Wind Your Mum Up

You can dawdle
You can whine
You can pull your mum away
You can drag her to a shop
You can swing her to and fro
You can annoy her
You can argue with her
You can force her to a shop
You can backchat her
You can put your foot down and say no
You can walk in front of her
You force her to go back to the car
You can make her buy stuff for you
You can make her get out of a shop
And you can get told off for that.

Jimmy Willis (7)
Haresfield CE Primary School, Stonehouse

Sports Day

Where's your kit
We need you, you're very fit
Don't worry there's a spare
It won't ruin your hair
Now go get your mates
After school you can have your dates.

Joe Hartshorn (10)
Haresfield CE Primary School, Stonehouse

Club Cool

Chewing gum in class,
Texting on my phone,
Isn't the message obvious?
I want to go home!
Getting into trouble,
Not listening about the Celts,
Are you blind? You cannot see,
I want to be somewhere else!
Scaring little kids
Sticking together like honey,
Finally told the teacher,
She didn't find it funny!
So here I am, in Miss' office,
Staring at the wall,
Feeling proud of myself
I'm now in club cool!

Esther Mounce (10)
Haresfield CE Primary School, Stonehouse

The Transparent Fella

Haunted house, big and creepy,
Cars come past, they're rather beepy.
Cobwebby corners, I can't believe it.
Is there a clean place? Not a bit.

Creepy-crawlies in the corner,
Shall we carry on? Can't think of anything mourner.
Along the corridor, up the stairs,
Dusty, slimy, horrible chairs.

Where could he be?
This transparent guy
In the bedroom low and high
Up in attic, down in the cellar
There he is, the transparent fella.

Harry Kirby (10)
Haresfield CE Primary School, Stonehouse

Cat Poem

Cats, cats, of all different kinds.
Cats, cats, how many can you find?
Cats, cats, fat and thin.
Cats, cats, in the bin.
Cats, cats, big and small.
Cats, cats, you know them all!

Ellie Card (10)
Haresfield CE Primary School, Stonehouse

Chocolate

I love chocolate, it tastes so nice,
I also love eating white chocolate mice,
I love it when the chocolate goes crunch,
But I don't usually have chocolate for lunch!

I hate when I go in the car,
My chocolate melts
My poor chocolate bar.

It comes in all different flavours
Like orange, chocolate and dark.
But when I give it to my dog
It makes him go crazy and bark.

Chocolate is so mouth-watering creamy
Eventually it makes me dreamy
When I eat chocolate
It makes me shout loud!
It feels like I am floating on a cloud.

Like I said before; I love chocolate
It is the best thing in the world!

Jessica Peart (10)
Hurst Primary School, Bexley

The Playground

Children's feet, tippy tap,
Rain falls, pitty pat.
I hear the whistle, loudly blow,
I say don't go.

Then I hear a cheer,
Children are very near.
Once again dancing with glee,
I join in happily.

Children's feet, tippy tap,
Rain falls, pitty pat.
It's time for children to go home,
I lay here on my own.

As I try to fall asleep,
I hear someone creep, creep.
What is it? What is it walking slow?
What is it? What is it I don't know!

It's a fox!
As quiet as a box
It's breathing slow,
I want it to go.

The children are back,
All wearing caps.
Ready for another day
Can't wait for them to play.

Jordan Bland (10)
Hurst Primary School, Bexley

Love

Love is a twinkle of moonlight.
Love is the smell of roses blooming.
Love is the sound of kittens purring.
Love is the taste of crackers and cheese.
Love is looking at the sunset.
Love reminds me of my family.
Love is like holding hands.
Love is like happiness.
Love is like a dream floating through the sky.
Love is like a horse galloping.
Love is like a rabbit hopping.
Love is like singing softly.
Love is like dancing across the sun.
Love is like shopping.
Love is like painting a picture.
Love is like midnight feasts.
Love is like shining stars.

Hannah Abrahams (10)
Hurst Primary School, Bexley

Winter

Winter is a time for love and care,
Winter is a time for people to share.
Winter is a time for presents and cards,
Winter cheers you can hear for yards and yards.

Winter is my favourite season,
And trust me it's for a good reason.
Winter is a time you have fun in the snow,
That is why it's my favourite you know.

Winter is lovely but ever so cold,
Winter is when you have to be bold.
Winter is when you sit by the fire,
Winter is when you can't be a liar.

Courtney Corcoran (10)
Hurst Primary School, Bexley

Fright Night!

On the 31st October,
When daytime is finally over.
Down goes the wicked sun
As we get ready for some fun!
There are some spooky Hallowe'en features,
And children as ghoulish creatures.
Some are monsters that are freakishly hairy,
And others that are just extremely scary.
At the stroke of midnight the moon will be bright,
And when you see the monsters you'll say,
'What a dreadful sight!'
So listen out for some vicious knocks at the door,
Kids trick or treating who might scare you to the core!
Later you may be feeling tired out,
From scaring everyone out and about.
The best thing to do is to head back home,
And your love of Hallowe'en has now been shown . . .

Grayce Durden (10)
Hurst Primary School, Bexley

Silence

Silence is where everything is quiet,
Silence is gloom and doom,
It's where people become silent,
With a zip upon their gloomy faces.

Silence is very peaceful,
Silence is a dove flying past you,
Silence is the colour white, white as a dove,
Silence is as peaceful as watching the snow drift on the ground.

Silence is as peaceful as flowers growing naturally,
Silence is like the trees standing still with no wind,
Silence is like birds gathering every berry.
Teachers are angry so they shout, 'Silence!' and that makes silence.

Fiona Burgess (10)
Hurst Primary School, Bexley

Untitled

The winter has come about
And the wind is in the trees.
The summer has passed
There's no more time for bees.
The snow has arrived with a winter breeze,
It has taken all the leaves off the trees.
The lake has frozen over with ice,
A cup of hot chocolate will make it feel nice.
The bitter, cold snow has covered the ground,
Look for the animals - there aren't any around.
The animals have all gone to hibernate,
Cos otherwise they'll freeze to death
They mustn't be late.
The snow looks so wonderful,
It sparkles in the sun,
All the little snowflakes,
Join together to make one.

Finlay Swain (10)
Hurst Primary School, Bexley

Love

Love, love
It's everywhere
It follows me around
Like I'm floating on air.

Love, love
It makes me blush
Everyone around me is in love.

Love, love
Everyone has it,
That is why you have a heart
To give out love,
And receive it back.

Alexa Terry (10)
Hurst Primary School, Bexley

Poetry Explorers 2009 - The South & South East

My Cat

The sun comes up for a lovely day,
And I go downstairs,
So I can play.
Who do I find lying on my hat?
I've been looking everywhere,
For my cat.

He cares and doesn't scratch or bite,
But he's sometimes afraid of heights.
It's a bit weird because he's like a dog,
But he sometimes acts like a lazy hog.

I can teach him tricks but only sometimes listens,
But a good thing is he makes things glisten.
I make him breakfast and for me,
And then we sip a cup of tea.

Tania Heckford (10)
Hurst Primary School, Bexley

Chocolate

I love chocolate, it tastes so nice;
I used to have chocolate mice.
When you take a bite,
A lot comes out, as quick as light.

I'm in Heaven,
With beautiful chocolate in Devon.
Tastes so nice when I take a crunch,
I usually get quite a chunk.

When you put it in your mouth,
It takes so long to melt, like sailing to the south.

It's fun to eat,
It tastes so nice,
Chocolate is the best thing *ever!*

Stephanie Holland (10)
Hurst Primary School, Bexley

Silence

Silence is the colour white
Sometimes golden, but always bright.
It smells of soap
It brings you hope.
Silence sounds like early dawn
When I wake, stretch and yawn.
Silence tastes like wafer,
Crispy and crunchy, just like paper.
Silence looks like an empty park
There are no miaows, there are no barks.
Silence feels like snuggling close
With a book you like the most.
Silence reminds me of the second before
Your favourite team is about to score.

Billy Cotterell (10)
Hurst Primary School, Bexley

Night

The moon is as bright as light;
It's scary,
It's creepy,
In the misty moonlight!

The shadows of cats strolling along the wall;
And the flapping of bats, looking for any bugs at all!
It's so quiet all around me,
Which makes me want to shout out loud,
As the moon is peeking over a very dark cloud!

The stars are twinkling,
And the moon is winking!
People are in bed,
Ready for the morning ahead!

Holly Morris (10)
Hurst Primary School, Bexley

Happiness

We're on our way to Lanzarote, aboard the aeroplane.
All around are smiling faces looking forward to the fun and games.
The doors are opened and wow, feel the heat.
Everybody is keen to get off, no one left in their seats.
We're on the coach, then off again, look it's the hotel.
I love being here on holiday, it's the best feeling in the world.

Yellow because it's bright and it makes you happy.
Candyfloss because it's sweet.
Children laughing because they're happy.
It tastes like my favourite chocolate
Everybody having a giant picnic at the park
Happiness feels like your softest jumper ever.

Ben Hubbard
Hurst Primary School, Bexley

Timé

What is that noise getting near?
What is it that we hear?
It is little feet, will we meet?
The door creeps open,
And who do I see?
My little sister doing a sneeze.
With red hair that gleams like the sun;
She's loads of fun.
She's got a big tum.
Like my mum.
Timé's got gleaming blue eyes;
And she likes yummy custard pies.

Niké Bester (10)
Hurst Primary School, Bexley

A Friendship Poem

A friend is someone special,
I think they are happy, funny people
who bring joy to everyone.
They are someone kind too.
Don't turn them away,
let them come to you and play.
Don't be horrible.
If you've had an argument,
try to say sorry
and it will go
away!

Emily Sieglar (10)
Hurst Primary School, Bexley

Fun (Funny Bunny)

Not all rabbits have funny habits
But my one does, he's mad.
His ears are long, his face is round
When he runs around he doesn't make a sound.
But when he's in his metal cage, he goes into a furious rage
And keeps me up all night.
In the night he gives me a fright and scares me half to death.
When he lies down, he has a funny frown,
And smiles when he does it.
All of this stuff is what makes him funny,
That's why I call him the funny bunny.

Ryan Traynor (11)
Hurst Primary School, Bexley

Love

Love is the colour of your red heart thumping in your chest.
The smell of love is the smell of bright red roses
being pressed into your hands by your loved one.
Love is the sound of the bride walking down the aisle
on her big day.
Love is that wonderful butterfly feeling building up in your stomach.
It's the taste of milky chocolate received from your anonymous lover.
Love reminds you of that day when you set your eyes on the right
person, the one forever.
Love is the look of angels above, peering down on all us precious
loved ones.

Isabelle Mary Penfold (11)
Hurst Primary School, Bexley

Love

Love is the colour of pink cushions.
It is like the smell of blossoms
Drifting through the air.
Love is the sound of peaceful music,
Harps playing gently.
It is the taste of sweet
Sweets melting in your mouth.
Love feels like warm blankets
Wrapping round you.
It looks like the beaming heart inside you.
Love reminds me of my family safe and sound.

Ellie-Mai Ford (9)
Hurst Primary School, Bexley

Happiness

The colour of happiness is yellow
Because it makes me feel mellow
It looks so bright
It could even be white.

Happiness is something I like
Because it sounds like my bike
That's when I taste the need
To feel excessive speed.

That's when I love the smell of rubber
When I'm off to see my lover.

Jean-Michel Breytenbach (10)
Hurst Primary School, Bexley

Love

The colour of love is red from our hearts.
The smell of love is the sweet scent of strawberry tarts.
The sound of love is the chime when your heart meets mine.
The taste of love is sweet red wine.
The look of love is the heart I see within your eyes.
The feel of love is when our hearts pound,
When it's time to say our goodbyes.
Love reminds me how happy I am when I am with you,
The person my heart belongs to.

The one I love!

Samantha Ford (10)
Hurst Primary School, Bexley

Fun

Fun is the colour of all the colours of the rainbow.
Fun is the smell of summer with all the flowers in bloom.
Fun is the sound of children playing in the park.
Fun is the taste of pizza and ice cream.

Fun is the sight of tea cups and Ferris wheels whirling round and round at the funfair.
Fun is the feel of the sun shining down on me
whilst riding my new bike for the first time.
Fun reminds me of a visit to Alton Towers for my 10th birthday surprise.

Alice Lydon (10)
Hurst Primary School, Bexley

Cricket

I feel nervous,
But yet excited,
As I get padded up,
For the first ball of the day.
The crowd are clapping
The crowd are shouting,
As I come onto the pitch just to play.
As I bowl the ball,
I see the stumps fall.
And everyone shouts, 'Out!'

Ben Murphy (10)
Hurst Primary School, Bexley

Love

Love is a shiny red, like a beautiful, pumping heart.
Love smells like a woman's posh perfume or a man's fresh cologne.
Love sounds like birds singing their sweet song,
Love tastes of a girl's strawberry lip gloss.
Love looks like dreamy eyes and a heart-stopping smile.
It feels all quivery inside, all nervous,
When that someone special holds you.
It reminds me of happy summer days.

Love is happiness.

Yasmin Badesha (10)
Hurst Primary School, Bexley

Joy Is . . .

Joy is black and white.
It smells of damp grass.
It sounds like the wind whistling.
Joy tastes like cotton wool.
It looks like a smooth ball of fur.
It feels like a fluffy scarf.
Joy reminds me of my dog Missie.
Missie used to chase cats.
She also chewed my favourite hats.

Andrew Ruane (10)
Hurst Primary School, Bexley

Fun

Fun is yellow buttercups and smells of flowers.
Fun is the sound of noisy children playing in the garden.
Fun tastes of ice cream and candyfloss from the shops.
Fun looks like a funfair and feels like you're on a roller coaster.
Fun reminds me of a hot summer's day on the beach.

Victoria Belk (11)
Hurst Primary School, Bexley

Joy

Joy is purple bridesmaid dresses going down the aisle.
Joy smells like Mum's home-made chocolate cupcakes coming out of the oven.
Joy sounds like my family cheering as England pick up the World Cup.
Joy tastes like brownies melting in your mouth slowly.
Joy feels like me cuddling my first teddy bear.
Joy looks like everybody smiling.
Joy reminds me of happiness on people's faces.

Rebecca Farrelly (9)
Hurst Primary School, Bexley

Going To A Football Match

We get to the ground and get a beer
When the players come out they get a cheer
We sing the club song,
When the player on our team gets a yellow card,
We usually think it's wrong.
When the other team score,
We just get one more.
When the final whistle goes, whether it is bad or good.
We sing all the way home.

Charlie Bagnall (11)
Hurst Primary School, Bexley

Peace

The colour of peace is orange, as the gleaming colour of a sunset.
Peace tastes like sweet Galaxy chocolate with crunchy red apples.
Peace sounds like harps playing quietly.
Peace feels like smooth and soft velvet.
Peace looks like a beach, the sea lapping at my heels.
Peace reminds me of World War II ending in harmony.

Lucy Harris (9)
Hurst Primary School, Bexley

Sadness

Black is the colour of death
Sadness is the smell of burned up ashes.
Sadness sounds like a terrible scream coming closer.
Sadness feels like something terrible.
Sadness reminds me of someone dying.
Sadness looks as awful as someone crying.
Sadness tastes like something black and burned.
Sadness is all of these.

Charlie Winter (10)
Hurst Primary School, Bexley

Fun

Fun, fun, fun, is as orange as the sun.
Fun, fun, fun, is fresh air at the seaside or going for a run.
Fun, fun, fun, it tastes of a caramel bun.
Fun, fun, fun, feels as light as a feather but not a massive tonne.
Fun, fun, fun, reminds me when I went to Alton Towers
but not when it was done.
Fun, fun, fun, looks like smiley faces
when the fun's only just begun.

Kaylee Heckford (10)
Hurst Primary School, Bexley

Fun

Fun is the colour of the sun shining in the sky.
Fun smells like cucumber, all fresh and new.
Fun sounds like the trees rustling in the wind.
Fun tastes like dark purple plums
all waiting to be the first ones to be eaten.
Fun looks like little boys and girls playing in a field.
Fun feels like you're swinging really high on a swing.
Fun reminds me of a burst of energy that makes you want to smile.

Olivia Ellen Leahy (10)
Hurst Primary School, Bexley

Cricket

As I hit the ball
It flew into the stands.
The crowd stood up
And clapped their hands.
As I bowled the ball,
I saw the stumps fall.
I shouted, Out!'
And the crowed cheered with a loud shout.

Conor Johnson (11)
Hurst Primary School, Bexley

Happiness

Happiness is a beam of sunshine in every soul,
It is the sound of laughter, ringing in my ears,
Happiness is the heavenly burst of flavour from my favourite dish.
Happiness is a contagious grin going all around the world.
It is a unique bright yellow from the tallest sunflower.
Happiness is the smell of a baking oven on a summer's day.
Happiness is your heart growing with joy and festivity.
It is the feeling of drifting to sleep in your new pyjamas.

Noémie Joelle Oster (10)
Hurst Primary School, Bexley

Joy

Joy is a blue sky
Joy is the smell of a butterfly
Joy is the sound of my mum's voice.
Joy is the taste of my dad's roast dinner.
Joy is the look of my mum's smiling face.
Joy is the feel of my mum's embrace.
Joy reminds me of when I was a baby boy
And that's joy.

Ben Dalton (10)
Hurst Primary School, Bexley

Pain

The colour of pain is red, like puddles of blood.
The scent of pain is the underground of Big Foot's den.
The sound of pain may be the Wicked Witch of the West's cackle.
The taste of pain is flesh and tonnes of meat.
Pain feels like a crab's shell too big for it.
It looks like the scariest horror film in history
It reminds me of shattered dreams and flesh-eating animals.
A wizard's treat!

Morgan Connell (9)
Hurst Primary School, Bexley

Happiness

Happiness is the colour gold.
Happiness is the smell of fresh air being given
Happiness is the sound of you and your friends cheering
because you won the football match.
Happiness tastes like lovely pepperoni pizza.
Happiness feels like friendship.
Happiness looks like the dazzling sun shining.
Happiness reminds me of my friends.

Kyle Anthony David Brown (9)
Hurst Primary School, Bexley

Fun

Fun is the colour of a rainbow in the sky,
Fun smells of lovely roses on your drive.
Fun sounds like children at a funfair,
Fun tastes like a lovely ripe pear.
Fun looks like a party hat I wear on my head,
Fun feels like my teddy bear I cuddle in bed.
Fun reminds me of playing in the snow,
When I jump in the swimming pool and watch the water flow.

Maisie Whittley (10)
Hurst Primary School, Bexley

Fun

Fun is the colour of an orange lamp glowing never endlessly.
It is the smell of fresh candyfloss,
Whisked around in a silver bowl.
Fun is the sound of a carousel packed with laughing children.
It is the taste of hot doughnuts being dropped into a paper bag.
Fun feels like a soft cushion, used for a pillow fight.
It looks like a smiling face, grinning up at me.
Fun reminds me of a noisy fairground.

Miranda Parkin (9)
Hurst Primary School, Bexley

Joy

Joy is like orange leaves falling from the trees.
Joy is the smell of sweets waiting to be eaten.
The sound of joy is music playing on the radio.
Joy is the taste of sweet strawberries
being picked off from the fields.
Joy feels like you want to jump around the room.
Joy looks like a smile being infected around the world.
Joy reminds me of dancing everywhere making people smile!

Abigail Stack (9)
Hurst Primary School, Bexley

Happiness

The colour of happiness is a blue sky in the middle of summer.
Happiness smells of a brand new classroom.
Happiness is when I hear the sound of children running around the playground, shouting and screaming.
The taste of happiness is lunch in the school hall.
It feels like opening my eyes for the first time.
Happiness looks like children having fun.
Happiness reminds me of walking for the first time.

Ezrie Cornford (9)
Hurst Primary School, Bexley

Fun

Fun is the colour of orange.
It smells like sweet fluffy candyfloss.
And sounds like children running up and down going, 'Yeah *woooooh!* oh boy this is a good one it tastes like ice cream.'
Fun makes me want to dance day till night.
Fun looks like the smile of a cheerful child.
And fun reminds me of children playing in a blossom tree in the hot, hot summer.

Brooke Connell (9)
Hurst Primary School, Bexley

Sadness

Sadness is the dark grey colour in the air on a misty night.
It's the sound of immense screaming.
Sadness looks like homeless, hungry people
on the streets of London.
It is the feeling of having no one to go to and nowhere to go.
Sadness smells of dry tears flowing onto the floor of a graveyard.
It reminds me of my relative dying.

Jacob Eller (10)
Hurst Primary School, Bexley

Pain

The colour of pain is dark red blood.
Pain is the smell of a rotting graveyard.
The sound of pain is a vampire screeching for blood.
The taste is like rotten seaweed and mouldy grasswater.
It feels like the stabbing of a new sharp knife.
The vision of pain is a fearsome wolf eating its prey.
Pain reminds me of someone being put into a coffin but screaming.

Emily Jenson (9)
Hurst Primary School, Bexley

Love

Love is like pink blossom on a tree on a summer's day.
The smell of love is a tree of pretty-smelling roses.
The sound of love is like peaceful music on a harp.
Love is sweet sherbet sinking into my mouth.
Love is like a pink, fluffy, cosy cushion.
Love looks like a colourful rainbow in the summer's sky.
Love reminds me of my family.

Emily Roffey (9)
Hurst Primary School, Bexley

Love

Love is pink, like marshmallows melting in my mouth
Love is the smell of freshly cut roses
Love sounds like a harp playing
Love tastes like melted chocolate
Love feels like a brand new mattress
Love looks like a newborn baby
Love reminds me of my two dogs.

Joe Williams (9)
Hurst Primary School, Bexley

My Red Sweet Love

My colour is red, like the red sky at night.
The smell is so lovely, like a red rose.
The sound of a heart beating, just like a clock.
And the taste of hot melted chocolate dribbling in your mouth.
It feels so good to be cared for and loved.
It reminds me of the colour red.
Red is for love.

Ellie May Collinson (10)
Hurst Primary School, Bexley

Joy

Joy is the colour of the coral reefs down under the sea.
Joy smells as fresh as green grass.
Joy is the sound of brass trumpets playing in an orchestra.
Joy tastes like gum balls that roll out of candy machines.
Joy feels like the excitement you feel before Christmas.
Joy looks like bright lights flashing on and off.
Joy reminds you of that cool summer breeze.

Emma Harris (9)
Hurst Primary School, Bexley

Peace

Peace is deep blue like the dark sky.
It is like the salty sea with the waves swishing from side to side.
Peace is lovely lemon cream.
It's like fluffy yellow chicks.
Peace is sheep munching grass.
It's like a field full of colourful flowers.
Peace is beautiful.

Tegan Battersby (9)
Hurst Primary School, Bexley

Anger

If anger was a colour it would be red.
It would be the smell of the school compost heap
If anger was a sound it would be the roar of a hungry lion.
It would be the taste of a horrible cold cucumber.
Anger feels like the rough sack against your leg.
Anger looks like someone trying to cut string that won't break.
It reminds me of a raging T-rex.

Tom Shea (9)
Hurst Primary School, Bexley

Love

Love is the colour of rose-pink,
It is the smell of gorgeous lavender candles,
Love is the sound of a cello playing in my mind,
It is the taste of creamy caramel chocolates,
Love feels like a soft, hairy cushion in bed,
It looks like pink blossom falling from a pink tree,
Love reminds me of my kind and loving family.

Emily Jenkins (9)
Hurst Primary School, Bexley

Love

Love is a colour of pink, soft, squishy marshmallows.
Love smells like walking into a perfume shop.
Love sounds like a love band performing on stage.
Love tastes like a chocolate cookie crumble melting in my mouth.
Love feels like my soft Arsenal duvet at night.
Love looks like my heart having a good time in Heaven.
Love reminds me of my family cuddled up on the soft sofa.

Harry Powley (9)
Hurst Primary School, Bexley

Fun

Fun is like an orange bouncy ball
Fun smells like sticky candyfloss
Fun sounds like children shouting joyfully
Fun tastes like the good hot dogs
Fun feels like a bouncy castle
Fun looks like the man that made the candyfloss
Fun reminds me of winning toys.

Savannah Golesworthy (9)
Hurst Primary School, Bexley

Love

The colour of love is like red roses drifting from side to side,
It smells of swirling hot chocolate.
Love is the sound of a harp playing peacefully.
It would be the taste of red shiny cherries.
Love feels like a comfy red cushion,
It looks like red-hot lava
And reminds me of my family.

Georgia Henry
Hurst Primary School, Bexley

Anger

Anger is the colour of hot red lava.
Anger is the smell of demon's flesh.
Anger is the sound of a vicious rhinoceros.
Anger is the taste of rotten apples.
Anger feels like cats scratching nervously.
Anger looks like a fire extinguisher.
Anger reminds me of a nail hitting continuously.

Ellie Owen (9)
Hurst Primary School, Bexley

Love

Love is the colour purple.
Love is the smell of red roses in someone's hand.
Love is the sound of harps playing in an orchestra.
Love feels like soft cosy bean bags sitting with you.
Love looks like flowers growing continuously.
Love reminds me of my friends playing nicely together again and again.

Eliane Newitt (9)
Hurst Primary School, Bexley

Love

Love is red rose petals just about to fall off a tree.
Love smells like blossom drifting through the air.
Love sounds like violins playing in the band.
Love tastes like strawberry cheesecake.
Love feels like a soft and cosy blanket on my warm bed.
Love looks like a beautiful heart.
Love reminds me of my family safe and sound.

Dylan Burke Taber (9)
Hurst Primary School, Bexley

Joy

The colour of joy is orange, like the sun
Joy smells like blueberry bubblegum
The sound of joy is children shouting, 'Whooooo!'
Joy tastes like fairy cakes
Joy makes me dance my socks off
Joy looks like children on the loop-da-loop,
Joy reminds me of the funfair.

Lauren Couldwell (9)
Hurst Primary School, Bexley

Love

Red is the colour of love
The smell of love is a strong scent of rose petals.
The sound of love is romantic music playing.
The taste of love is sweet strawberries.
Love feels like sponge.
Love looks like a heart.

Isaac Sam Mitchell (9)
Hurst Primary School, Bexley

Sunset

It's flaming hot,
Like a big red pot,
It lights up the sky,
With its big red eye,
Could you fly as high?

Taylor Whittley (10)
Hurst Primary School, Bexley

If

I've found something, a wonderful thing
And I'll give you a clue but I can't tell you.

This thing can blow Mount Everest apart
and help you make a huge start.
If you want to . . .

I've found something, a wonderful thing
And I'll give you a clue but I can't tell you.

It can cut through rock with a single slice
and make you have a never-ending life.
If you want to . . .

I've found something, a wonderful thing
And I'll give you a clue but I can't tell you.

This thing can even give lions a fright
and make you dead in the middle of the night,
If you want to . . .

I've found something, a wonderful thing
And I've given you a clue but I'll *never* tell *you!*

Holly Olivia Hodgson (10)
Killigrew Primary & Nursery School, St Albans

Maybe One Day . . .

Maybe one day I'll go up to space
Or be a great mechanic
Be a dentist who gives you your brace
Or an expert on the Titanic
I long to be a farmer
But I'd beg to be an actor
Or work in the zoo with a llama
But I think I've got the X Factor.

Maybe one day I'll be a bread baker
Or at a pinch a taxi driver
But maybe a Top Trumps card maker
Though I could be a scuba-diver
Maybe I'll be an illustrator
Though I was born to be a lawyer
Perhaps a caring waiter
I could even be an employer.

Maybe one day I'll be a pilot,
Someday I'll be prime minister
A head teacher, like Miss Mylotte
Perhaps a spy, that's much more sinister
Maybe I'll be a writer
Though I'd rather be a vet
Perhaps a kung fu fighter
I could be an army cadet.

Maybe one day I'll be a surveyor
I could choose to be an optician
I could even be a drum player
I could be an electrician
Maybe I'll be a fancy chef
Though I could be a barber
Or an angry football ref
Or the bloke that works at the harbour!

I only get one choice of job
So which to choose?
I just don't know!

Jack Mackey (10)
Killigrew Primary & Nursery School, St Albans

What If . . .

What if my clocks jumped off the shelf, chose a partner and started dancing the salsa?
What if the china cats sang at the tune of my wooden xylophone?
What if my bookshelf recommended a book when
I was feeling down?
What if my colouring books took away the colour from my bedroom?
What if my wardrobe threw out the clothes he wanted me to wear?

What if . . .

What if my radio started playing really loudly so the wooden spoons could boogie the night away?
What if my teddy bear jumped out of the basket and enjoyed the evening sunset?
What if my dolls hopped over the bookshelf and read each of my favourite story books?
What if my desk tried to encourage me while doing homework?
What if my bed hummed a lullaby when I couldn't get to sleep?

What if all this could happen?

Laura Payton (10)
Killigrew Primary & Nursery School, St Albans

Morning Rise

Branches huddle together, trapping in the warmth.
The river trickles passionately, carefully dodging the treacherous rocks.
Frost glints in the early morning sunshine, eagerly waiting to melt away from the brightness.
Early birds gather together their choir
and begin their first lulling song.
Undergrowth listens to the violently howling wind.
Wind pursues the darkness away whilst the sun begins to tell the story of the day.

Now morning has come.

Isabel Craven (10)
Killigrew Primary & Nursery School, St Albans

Happiness

Happiness is a baby panda climbing through the bamboo
to his mother.
Happiness is like a blossom blooming in the sweet-smelling breeze.
Happiness is like the sun dipping down into the distance.
Happiness is warmth that will never leave you.
Happiness will stay forever and ever.

Happiness is like a soft pillow filled with feathers
hugging you gently.
Happiness is a birthday giving you a wish and a pinch of luck.
Happiness is family helping you discover new things each day.
Happiness is a gift filled with surprises.
Happiness will stay forever and ever.

Happiness is Christmas wishing you the best ever year.
Happiness expresses many emotions.
Happiness is love filling you up every day.
Happiness is your friends, there for you when you're down.
Happiness *will* stay!

Natasha Wai Ling Chen (11)
Killigrew Primary & Nursery School, St Albans

Morning Is Here

Bare bristly trees sway in the gentle breeze,
Dancing to the early morning birdsong,
Dew-covered grass shivers,
Trying to shake off the clingy coat of frost that makes it shine,
A swirling river pushes its way forward through the undergrowth,
Glistening in the rays of sunlight appearing over the horizon,
Leaves stop prancing in the pools of moonlight and lie down,
Once more a crunchy carpet of colours.
Beams of sunlight cover the hills, gripping
And pulling at the grass imprisoned in frost,
The sun is out and shining,
Morning is here.

Philippa Jane Boxford (10)
Killigrew Primary & Nursery School, St Albans

The Moor/Emotions

Wind whistles over the moor,
Snow-capped mountains shiver in the darkness,
Bracken catches against each other, the only sound there is,
River sits there for eternity as the ice freezes every drop of water,
Dragonflies glint every time the moonlight hits their body.
As time goes by, the sun starts to seep through the clouds,
Cockerels count the seconds then start the wake up call.
Hedgehogs' eyes open up to the daylight sun,
Birds sing the bird song, finally,
It's day . . .

Love is the sweet smell of apple crumble which has just finished cooking,
Hate is the spicy hot, fiery taste of chillies making their way down your throat,
Joy is finding your name written on the Nobel Prize,
Envy is the green, mouldy cheese that has been sitting in the fridge for months, these are my emotions and this is what I feel.

Eleanor Webster (10)
Killigrew Primary & Nursery School, St Albans

The Kitchen

It's noon
It's all quiet in the Connor household
Suddenly a fight awakes
But . . . an enormous fight awakes
What if the saucepan wobbles loudly to fight with his best friend?
What if the tap cries to distract the plates to be washed?
What if the table has a wobbling fight with the chair?
What if the hot, spicy Indian food has a vicious fight with chocolate cake?
What if the knife has a weeping contest with the silver shiny fork?
What if the tea towel has a scramble with the wooden spoon?
What if the juice carton has a hissy fit with the cloudy, mouldy milk?

Bethany Connor (10)
Killigrew Primary & Nursery School, St Albans

What If . . .

It was night-time in the Shaw house when downstairs in the living room, a party awoke.
What if the grey telly shook as the music came screeching on?
What if the funky chair went to sleep because it got bored looking at people dance?
What if the flowery curtains smashed the window as they were swaying?
What if the wooden table started to jiggle when he heard the pumping music?
What if the fluffy cushion danced with the grey telly?
What if the cute teddy was dancing in its colourful dreams?
What if the black shoes started to move as the jewellery box opened in surprise!
Then suddenly the sun shone through the smashed window and whispered, 'Come on and fix the window and crawl back to your places for another day?'

Chantelle Lilly Shaw (10)
Killigrew Primary & Nursery School, St Albans

What If . . .

It's midnight
Everybody is asleep but the kitchen?
What if the eggs fly across the room, like someone kicking a football high in the sky?
What if the spoons dig their way out of the draw like moles?
What if the knives come out the drawer and start fighting
like knights in shining armour?
What if the radio starts going crazy as the music comes out?
What if the washing machine chucks out clothes
and jigs to the beat?
What if the toaster makes toast fly out?
Then the disco lights turn off and everything cleans up and crawls back to its normal place.
All is quiet once more.

Alistair Wyllie (10)
Killigrew Primary & Nursery School, St Albans

What If?

What if my light up alarm clock got up
and sang in front of my very eyes?
What if my books went OCD and tidied my room for me?
What if my lamp morphed into a disco ball
and couldn't stop spinning with joy?
What if my door told me all the answers to my homework over
and over?
What if my teddies took up hip-hop dancing together and my amp
went booming mad?
What if my book became a famous author?
What if my duvet grew legs and danced the night away with my
pillows to the sound of my heartbeat.
What if my lamp taught my squeaky floorboards to sing?
What if my shoe learnt to run and went to the 2012 Olympics?

What if . . . ?

Gabi Zöe Taylor (10)
Killigrew Primary & Nursery School, St Albans

What If?

What if my Lego plane started its engines and flew around my room like a crazy hover bird going mental?

What if one of my comic books said, 'See you later,' grabbed a suitcase and ran to work?

What if three of my pencils started doing the Irish dance,
Like the pros performing to 30,000 people?

What if all my books climbed on my book shelf and dropped off one by one and parachuted like a daredevil?

What if my little teddy tried to trampoline on my bed?

What if my remote control car started driving away from my toy tank like a mental car thief?

What if all this were true? I would have the messiest room ever.

Harry James Charles Reeves (11)
Killigrew Primary & Nursery School, St Albans

What Is Pink?

What is pink?
A rose is pink, as it sways in the wind.
What is red?
A strawberry's red and with sugar tastes just right.
What is orange?
A satsuma's orange skin and inside too.
What is white?
A cloud is white, unless there's lots of rain in it.
What is yellow?
A lemon's yellow and sour too.
What is green?
The grass is green, just the grass.

Sam Lachau (10)
Killigrew Primary & Nursery School, St Albans

The Most Amazing Sight

The sun pushes with all his might as he catapults beams of light to please the others.
The sky is gently drifting along as she thinks everyone is happy,
The mountain slyly creeps closer, trying not to disturb anyone,
The snow cap melts in the sunshine while calling for help,
The canyon sunbathes as it calmly whistles to itself,
The sand slithers silently across the canyon like an undercover spy,
The trees pray for survival as they are pounded by landslides whilst exposed to the burning heat of the searing sun
The branches sway to the sound of the canyon's soft, uplifting melody,
As the leaves fan themselves to disperse the sweltering heat.

Ronan Thomas Harris (10)
Killigrew Primary & Nursery School, St Albans

What If?

It's midnight.
The Bramwells are fast asleep, but not in the living room because it's come alive.

What if the dog sang 'Hound Dog' as the music thumped out?
What if the laptop danced and twirled across the floor?
What if the funky green Hoover whizzed into the chunky sofa?
What if the chinchilla slid across the table?
What if the cat jumped on the drum set?
What if the TV screamed as the music came into its speakers?
What if the phone rang with joy?
Just then, the sun said good morning and all was great once more.

Beatrix Julia Adelina Bramwell (10)
Killigrew Primary & Nursery School, St Albans

What If . . .

It is morning in the Wells' household
I get up for school but in the bathroom a party awakes,
What if my toilet mat grabs the dancing sink?
What if the angry toilet brush is hitting the happy bath to death?
What if the wooden cupboard opens and closes
as all the stuff falls out?
What if the slimy shampoo is sliding down the shiny bath?
What if the scary shower is going mad spraying everything?
What if the mad bath jumps up and down?
What if the crazy shower curtain is flapping on the floor?
I get back from school and all the things go back in their places.

Oliver Wells (10)
Killigrew Primary & Nursery School, St Albans

Love Is . . .

Love is an elegant, peaceful bird soaring through the air like a shooting star.
Joy is the relaxing sea gently swaying in the beautiful sunset.
Pain is a vampire digging its teeth into my heart.
Sadness is a thousand dead flowers watching over a swamp of thick mud.
Happiness is beautiful fireworks rising and falling in the moonlight.
Excitement is a playful monkey actively swinging through vines.
Anger is a fearsome lion scampering across the burning sun, chasing an unfortunate zebra.
Fear is a ghost floating towards a spooky house.

Jessica Jabbitt (10)
Killigrew Primary & Nursery School, St Albans

What If . . .

It's late in the Aldridge household
The lights are out, everybody is in bed, tired and asleep
But bad things happen in Luke's room.

What if the chair glances at the bed as if to pounce?
What if the drawers stare in surprise?
What if the TV gets up and runs around the room?
What if the Scalextrix starts speeding round the track?
What if the carpet grabs the TV in anger and shakes it?
What if the door strikes the handle to escape?
What if the mini BMX does a back flip on the shelf?

Luke Aldridge (10)
Killigrew Primary & Nursery School, St Albans

A Winter Morning

Shivering strands of grass weakly shake the frost off their tips.
The great shining sun instils its light on each spindly branch.
Snowdrops emerge from the undergrowth to show their faces.
Frolicky newborn rabbits stagger their way out of their warm cosy homes.
Squirrels shake their red bushy tails proudly and nibble at previously collected nuts.
A river flows slowly, pushing its way through cracking ice.
Clouds pass dreamily, not bothering about their shapes.
A robin hops into view, pecks at a berry and disappears.

Eleanor Friend (10)
Killigrew Primary & Nursery School, St Albans

They Are . . .

Dad,
He is a calm wave carrying me upshore,
He is a helpful star guiding me along,
Mum,
She is a sturdy pillar supporting me forever
She is an enjoyable book giving me fresh ideas,
They are,
They are a joyful duo helping me see everything good,
They are an inspiring novel, filling my mind.

Emily Smith (10)
Killigrew Primary & Nursery School, St Albans

Feelings

Hate is a fiery dragon rampaging inside my angry head.
Envy is a poisonous snake wrapping itself tightly around my twisted stomach.
Joy is a colourful rainbow sliding brightly in my big fluttering eyes.
Love is a roller coaster whizzing quickly down my tingling spine.

Daniel Salter (10)
Killigrew Primary & Nursery School, St Albans

A Magical Morning At The Moor

Moist, wet undergrowth blows in the gentle breeze,
White watercress is dripping with droplets of fresh rain.
Tall trees stand, moving freely to the sound of the birds' song.
The moon pulls the snoring sun up from its rest and into the red sky,
past the cloud-men who follow darkness.
The moving river sits by the undergrowth, being the home of Jack
and Jill, two energetic frogs.
Bare blazes of grass enter the fillets of day.
A flower petal of joy falls on the deprived area of silence . . .

Josephine Ashenhurst (10)
Killigrew Primary & Nursery School, St Albans

As The Day Dawns

The sun dances along the horizon at the start of dawn.
The river rushes peacefully through the morning breeze.
The undergrowth sways gently in the wind.
The clouds push calmly through the sky.
The leaves of the trees are frozen like ice on a cold winter's day.
The branches of the trees look like melted chocolate.
The twigs and sticks on the floor go *crunch! crunch!*
When you step on them.
What a beautiful morning.

Eleanor Wright (10)
Killigrew Primary & Nursery School, St Albans

Things

He is a ferocious lightning going wild in the air.
She is a lonely bear sitting silently on the shivering street.
Hate is charging lions gnashing their sharp, long teeth.
Love is a powerful eagle as it spreads its wings across the clear, red, hot sky.
Joy is a beautiful butterfly with the most graceful pattern ever.

Chloe Cocks (10)
Killigrew Primary & Nursery School, St Albans

Love I Can't Explain

Love is like a roller coaster soaring through the dreamy horizon.
Love is like a plane dipping in and out of the gentle clouds.
Love is like a fairy-tale fantasy with dreams you can't imagine.
Love I can't explain.

Love is like a flower petal floating through the calm breeze,
Love is like a red rose with all its passion and desire,
Love is like a pounding heart that shares its wonderful emotions,
Love I can't explain.

Megan Karen Ann Goalen (10)
Killigrew Primary & Nursery School, St Albans

The Winter's Closing In

The undergrowth danced through the damp slippery mud.
The murky water slithered along the riverbed and bank.
The clouds crawled across the misty sky above.
The trees grew bare because winter was at its peak.
The grass got ice drops on their tiny little petals.
The river's flow got slower and slower because of the icy days.
The winter's closing in on us, the winter's closing in.

Rebecca Carter (11)
Killigrew Primary & Nursery School, St Albans

Riverbank

Sky pursues the sun into the early morning,
River trickles to the beat of the bird song,
Undergrowth sways in the cold fresh wind,
Frost disintegrates by the fierce beam of sun.

Emma Joy Leto (10)
Killigrew Primary & Nursery School, St Albans

The Careless World

The careless world
You can never trust
This dangerous world
You can never count on

This careless world
Brings you down
Whenever you're happy
You will frown

The powerful earthquakes
Destroy the villages
People always sobbing
People always sighing

The careless world
You can never trust
This dangerous world
You can never count on

The villages are abandoned
With nobody left
People pray
People pray!

Nour Chaouaytarav (10)
Mandeville Primary School, St Albans

The Racing Car

The racing car is as fast as a lightning bolt,
With a design hand-carved like an angel.
The colour's dark purple like a stormy day,
And with spinners on each side of the car
And a never-ending battery and engine,
With cells hand-carved on the boot of the car.
Nobody will see it's a cheater.

Lascell Isaac Maher (10)
Mandeville Primary School, St Albans

The Dreadful Rain And Thunder

The rain clatters like hooves on roofs,
The clouds' tears shower the whole city,
It falls like little droplets,
And stomps like an elephant.

It shimmers like glitter,
It cackles like thunder,
And it's fierce like a lion,
And fast like a cheetah.

The thunder is sharp as a knife,
It knocks on people's windows,
It stings like a bumblebee,
And it is bright like the sun.

Dreadful rain, dreadful rain, go away,
Come back another day.

Thunder, thunder go away,
Go to another city,
And never come back.

Najiyah Ali (10)
Mandeville Primary School, St Albans

Earthquake

Once there was an earthquake
It was so dangerous
Humans died, houses collapsed,

The rescue team were astonished
All they could do was weep in despair
And look at the damage that was made,

People could not believe their house was gone
They would not sleep in their home
People felt lonely.

Harry Henderson (11)
Mandeville Primary School, St Albans

The Annoying Earthquake

People are living hard,
It is traumatising and sad,
The injuries are like a fox eating a bird,
They are really worried so they don't live in their houses,

O' how bad can it be?
Watching people suffer and die can be so hard to see,
Everyone knows some people are poor,
But they don't really care anymore,

People are living hard,
The weather is disgraceful,
The thunderstorm is as petrifying as a lion,
So it wouldn't be good if you are strolling about,

O' how bad can it be?
I'm happy it wasn't me,
So much suffering in this world,
That's what I've been told.

Nahida Chowdhury (10)
Mandeville Primary School, St Albans

The Train And The Noise

The train was whistling through the air
Some people did not know what the noise was,
The wind was whistling a mournful tune,
The tune was coming from the sky,
Some people thought it was the train.

The fruit that it would be is a tomato
Because it is red and soft.
The building is a skyscraper,
Because it is very tall and wide,
The type of vehicle it would be is a Lamborghini,
Because trains go extremely fast.

Keely Jayne Hardman (10)
Mandeville Primary School, St Albans

Help The Poor Survive

Think they have nothing
They don't have homes
People sob out there
People are terrified that their children will pass away
Please help them survive.

Children don't have enough shelter
Children starve
Adults worry
People die
Children lose their family nearly every day
Please help them survive.

Think, think, what do you have?
Think, think, what do they have?
Please, please give them food
Please, please help them survive.

Charlotte O'Connell (10)
Mandeville Primary School, St Albans

SOS

My stomach is moaning for many days, SOS
I have to walk barefooted everywhere, SOS
I need a roof to live under, SOS
My child shivers as the cold wind brushes
against her rosy red cheeks at night, SOS
Gradually, my child is dehydrating, SOS
I beg the rich to give food to the poor, SOS
They grey cloud sheds its tears on me, SOS
A pinch full of rice is a meal a day for me and my child, SOS
I never see my child laugh, she is alone, SOS
The time has come for me to execute my child
As she will have a pleasant time in Heaven, SOS.

Save Our Souls.

Fariha Qureshi (10)
Mandeville Primary School, St Albans

Help These People

We are so lucky to have a home, but some are not so lucky,
Help these people!
Us children have a family, but some people don't
Help these people!
Some people have pleasant homes, but some don't,
Help these people!
We have so much delicious food every day, but some don't,
Help these people!

Now there has been a colossal earthquake, people are dying,
They have no homes, no food and some people are even missing.
So help these people!

Saiyara Choudhury (10)
Mandeville Primary School, St Albans

My Friend

My friend is like a light that flickers on in the night,
But when he's angry, he roars like a lion,
When he walks along the street, he waddles like a penguin,
When he's calm, he soars in the sky like a kite,
He can run as fast as a cheetah.

He sings with a voice like an angel
He's as cuddly as a teddy bear,
He's as smart as a book that knows everything,
But when he's tired he moves as slowly as a snail.

Louis Hollands (11)
Mandeville Primary School, St Albans

No Help

Homeless people have no help,
They can't go anywhere and still no help,
People stuck with no money have no help,
People dying and getting no help.

Nothing to eat and still no help,
People with no houses have no help,
People sleeping while rain pours have no help,
Children with no mums and dads have no help.

Ihsan Zaman (10)
Mandeville Primary School, St Albans

Silence

Silence
Silence is white, as white as snow,
Silence smells of the wind whistling past your nose.
Silence feels soft and cool,
Silence is tears, time and thought.
Silence is sweet and sometimes sour,
Silence sounds smooth and still,
Silence reminds me of sadness.

Anger
Anger is red, as red as a rose,
Anger smells horrid, like rotten eggs,
Anger feels rough and sharp,
Anger looks ugly, ugly as a devil,
It tastes sour, sour as a lemon,
Anger sounds loud and ear-piercing,
Anger reminds me of an empty feeling and loneliness.

Emilia Smith (10)
Mortimer St Mary's School, Reading

Fun

Fun looks like children at a birthday party, screaming and having a good time.
Adults sitting down and catching a nap.
Sunbathing by a beach with children in the water, splashing each other with joy.

Fun reminds me of my seventh birthday party, eating cupcakes with my friends, in the cosiness of my own garden.
Shouting to my family from the warm, turquoise, sparkling water in Turkey.

Fun sounds like the fun at a beach, the shouts at a park and the first miaow of newborn kittens, playing in your bedroom!

Fun is a rainbow of bright, happy colours,
Red, pink, yellow, blue, gold, purple, silver, green and lots more.
The colour of the sun on a sunny day, the water at a beach and the grass shining on the dawn of a new day.

Fun smells of cake at a party, of dew at the beginning of a fun new day.
The smell of burning at a camp, toasting marshmallows with all your friends.

Fun feels warm and good inside, it's what makes you feel happy on that wet, rainy day.

Fun tastes like the icing on a cake at a child's birthday party, the saltwater of the sea on a sunny day,
The taste of breakfast at the beginning of that fun, sunny morning,
The softness and warmth of freshly toasted marshmallows.

Sophie James (10)
Mortimer St Mary's School, Reading

Silence

Silence is white, like the world is frozen and nothing is happening.
It seems to put a bland taste in your mouth and makes your mouth feel dry and lost.
Silence is black, like standing on the pavement in the dark with heavy rain pounding on your back.
Silence is grey, it is a grey cloud hovering over your head with you standing isolated under it.
It is dull and boring.
Silence reminds you of screaming from the prison cell,
Screams of sheer terror and fright.
Screams of people who know they have done wrong.
Silence looks like nobody can speak, that everyone has been silenced and are looking at each other in desperation.
Silence smells of nothing! Nobody moves, nobody speaks.
It is like the warm summer sun shining on the silent playground
After all the kids have gone home.

Helen Fraser (10)
Mortimer St Mary's School, Reading

Joy

Flowers that smell like a dream and fresh grass on the hills
That's the smell of joy.
The rainbow like red, pink, green. That is the colour of the rainbow.
The kids playing with toys in the park and happy faces.
That is what it looks like.
Your feet have no shoes, your feet are on the grass,
It feels beautiful and there is a race going on.
You have come first in the race, that is what it feels like.
People are singing and laughing so happily,
That is what it sounds like.
Butterflies lifting me up in the air so I can see the world.
That is what it reminds me of.
Sweets, so sweet in the sun.

Jenny Foy (10)
Mortimer St Mary's School, Reading

Terror

Terror is a thunderous creature with a dangerous smell to its name
Like a dark, disgusting animal that slumbers in the depths of Hell.
Terror is steam, like ugly orcs snorting and fighting the warriors with the foul sound of death.
Terror sounds like chalk on a blackboard.

Terror is trouble and screams and has a look of evil red eyes and unshaven, smelly hairs around the nostrils and below.
Terror is black, like a thunder cloud, but then suddenly striking its evil lightning in a flash and then goes back into the darkness.
Terror is a reminder of Hell where evil hovers.
It reminds you of anything dark and terrifying.
Terror is sandpaper rubbing roughly against the skin as the nail breaks through the bloody skin with a scream.
Terror has a taste that no man or woman can eat.
Terror is broccoli.

Toby Payne (10)
Mortimer St Mary's School, Reading

What Is Love?

Love feels like a very big smile.
Love can go as far as the Nile.
Love tastes like a chocolate cake.
Love is the colour of a bright blue lake.

Love sounds like a busy celebration.
Run by the people who invited the nation.
Love will remind you of the things you like.
Your house, your pet, your scooter, your bike.

Love looks like a group of friends.
Playing where the river bends.

I've written a poem and it's almost through,
For that's what love means to me.
What does love mean to you?

Emily Scott (10)
Mortimer St Mary's School, Reading

Pain

Pain is red, like when someone smacks your bare skin,
Pain is black, like when you get a scab.
Pain looks like a dull, freezing morning,
Pain looks like the farmer's face when he cooks his beloved chicken.

Pain sounds like a child, starving to death,
Pain sounds like a soldier in battle, killing his best friend,
Pain smells like a jail cell that hasn't been cleaned for years,
Pain smells like someone who hasn't washed for years.

Pain reminds you of a loved one that died.
Pain reminds you of all the bad things you have done.
Pain feels like you are going to die,
Pain feels like you will never love again.

Pain tastes like cold, soggy cabbage,
Pain tastes like a raw egg.

Linzi Asher (10)
Mortimer St Mary's School, Reading

What Is Love?

Love looks colourful and bright like flowers with hearts.
So bright it can blind you.
The pink for beauty, the white for safety, blue for security.

It feels like a long journey through happiness, emotions exploding everywhere shivering down your body and you forget everything bad.

It sounds like a long-lasting sound of laughter from children.

It reminds my mind of roses filling my brain, with some time, they turn into thoughts.
What would the world be without love?

Love smells like melted chocolate, I can almost taste it.

Love tastes like strawberries, sometimes sweet and sometimes sour
But love lasts more than an hour.

Zhanaye Fenty (10)
Mortimer St Mary's School, Reading

Fun

Fun sounds like the tropical blue ocean.
Fun sounds like people at a concert, it is as loud as the biggest hurricane and as loud as the most silent moth.
Fun feels like all the evil in the world has been sucked up and can't come back.
Fun is the deepest blue, the goldest gold, the brightest yellow,
The whitest white, the most beautiful jungle, the brightest desert.
Fun reminds you of the happiest moments of your life and the most exciting moments of your life.
Fun smells like lavender, fun smells like roses, fun smells like honey, fun smells like golden syrup.
Fun tastes like the juiciest watermelon, the ripest apple, the sweetest plum.
Fun looks like the sun, fun looks like diamonds, fun looks like the full moon, fun looks like honey.

Jake Sainsbury (10)
Mortimer St Mary's School, Reading

Happiness

Happiness looks like birds dancing in the sky, a running gazelle and a trickling stream.
Happiness feels like being wrapped up in a thick cotton blanket on a cold night.
Happiness is a warm friendly yellow, as warm as the sun on a hot day.
Happiness reminds me of a tropical island bursting with wildlife.
Happiness smells like a new-baked cake just come out of the oven.
Happiness tastes of toffee when its taste is best and creamy.
Happiness sounds like birds tweeting, a song in the morning as the sun comes up.

James Bridgland (10)
Mortimer St Mary's School, Reading

Joy

Joy is blue, like the beautiful sunny morning.
Joy is yellow, like the warmth of the sun drifting up your nose.
Joy is green, like greenery surrounding you from side to side.
Joy is purple, not a boy's colour and not a girl's colour,
It is all colours like us!
Joy is pink, like two girls wearing the same pink dresses
walking down the park's path.
Joy is brown, like a brown sandcastle standing in front of you,
One minute it is standing bold and strong, but the next minute it has
been washed away by the sea.
Joy is red, like the sea salt drifting into your thirsty mouth.

Aqsa Aziz (10)
Mortimer St Mary's School, Reading

Joy Is Wonderful

Joy is red, a little dab of love,
Joy is pink, a teaspoon of happiness,
Joy is gold, a bucket of kindness,
Joy is blue, a hand of sharing,
Joy is the smell of wonderful daisies,
Joy is a feeling of happiness,
Joy is a remembrance of your family,
Joy is a taste of juicy strawberries,
Joy is an eye of a loved one,
Joy is a look of a wonderful rose,
Joy has a wonderful feeling and makes everyone happy!

Louisa Collins (10)
Mortimer St Mary's School, Reading

What Is Silence?

Silence is silent
Silence is not colourful
Its colour is black, white,
Clear and grey.

Silence is no noise,
Quiet as anything.

Silence feels like a
Soft and calm feeling
Like no other feeling,
It is possibly boring.

Joe Margetts (10)
Mortimer St Mary's School, Reading

Pain

Pain feels bad, it feels like everyone and everything in the world is going to crumble, until you realise that someone is there to help you.
Pain is a black or a dark grey.
Pain sounds like a dead man screaming in his coffin.
Shaking and rolling around like a crying zombie.
Pain tastes like blood that has just been vomited up
and swallowed back down.
Pain reminds me of when I broke my arm.
Pain smells like an old dead skeleton that has been there for centuries.

Christopher Harris (10)
Mortimer St Mary's School, Reading

What Is Fun?

I think fun looks like happiness and playing.
Fun reminds me of the Lego Indiana Jones game and Club Penguins.
It smells of food because you smell food when you're playing.
Fun does not taste of anything.
I think fun is red.
I think the sound of my PSP and when I drop something is the sound of fun.
Fun feels like running around with my friends.
Fun is fun.

Ryan Riddle (11)
Mortimer St Mary's School, Reading

Happiness

Happiness looks like a big face with a massive smile on it.
Happiness feels like a massive cuddle from someone you love.
Happiness reminds me of people laughing about on a nice sunny day.
Happiness smells of the clean fresh air.
Happiness tastes like a chocolate with chocolate sauce in it or pancakes covered in golden syrup.
Happiness is orange and yellow for the big bright sun with a touch of green for the full park.
Happiness sounds like birds tweeting on a bright Saturday morning.

William Bray (10)
Mortimer St Mary's School, Reading

What Is Anger?

Anger, blacks and greys and vibrant reds,
Is like when you get anger in your head.
It feels like you want to take it out
With people who are about.

Stephen Gomm (11)
Mortimer St Mary's School, Reading

Wonder

Wonder is a pale sea-blue, like the colour of the sea on the horizon.
Wonder is like a delicate yellow flower in a meadow of gently waving grass.
Wonder is like a pale violet bird humming in the background.
Wonder is like a bowl of sweet, fresh, red strawberries in thick cream.
Wonder is like being high up in the lush green rainforests with the song of all the birds of paradise.
Wonder is like the gentle brushing of the long green grass against your legs.
Wonder is like a pool of deepest sea-blue.

Emily Lowe (11)
Mortimer St Mary's School, Reading

What Is Pain?

Butterflies in your tummy,
A punch round the face.
The taste of torture is not nice.

The colours red and black,
Red for vain, black for pain.
It gives you strain,
You'll hate the pain.

Bad news is coming,
You better get running.

Lauren Jury (10)
Mortimer St Mary's School, Reading

Love

Love is red, like a heart full of love with kisses.
It feels like lots of love in you and happiness.
It sounds romantic and tasty.

Chloe O'Rourke (10)
Mortimer St Mary's School, Reading

Pain

Pain is white, like the colour of your face when you are ill.
Pain tastes like something that you've just eaten or drunk that's sour like cranberry juice.
Pain reminds me of war and fighting.
Pain sounds like a piercing scream from someone that's being chased by something unknown in the middle of the night.
Pain feels like someone has just punched you in the stomach.
Pain smells like a skunk that's just come right up to you.
Pain looks like a ghost in the middle of the darkest night.

Anna Hewison (10)
Mortimer St Mary's School, Reading

What Is Love?

Love is as smooth as a flat stone.
Love is as squidgy as a foam ball.
Love smells as clean as soap and fresh water.
Love looks like a calm blue wave.
Love is a sound of peace and harmony.
Love tastes like sweet and sour tropical fruits from amazing islands.
Love's colour is what you choose it to be.
Love reminds you of a happy time and the people who are lovely and kind.

Hamish Patterson (10)
Mortimer St Mary's School, Reading

What Is Fun?

Fun is vastly soft like velvet,
Fun is as tasty as a chicken fillet.
Fun is jolly and brings you joy,
Fun makes you happy, like receiving a toy.
Fun is a lolly that you are licking,
And it makes me feel like a fun-loving chicken.

Abigail Cottingham (10)
Mortimer St Mary's School, Reading

Love

Love is yellow, like my family having fun in the garden when the sun is shining.
Love is purple, like the sound of rain pouring down onto the ground.
Love is green, like when my mum hugs me happily.
Love is white, like when I play in the snow with my friends and family.
Love is red, like the taste of sweets oozing in my mouth.
Love is colourful, like the animals at the zoo playing in their enclosures.
Love is fresh, like the air around us.

Emily Pickett (10)
Mortimer St Mary's School, Reading

What Is Terror?

Terror is black, because it is dark like when you go in a room where the light switch won't work.

It is painful and fearful.
Terror is ugly like a snail.
Terror sounds creepy like a haunted house.

Terror tastes bitter, you would have to spit it out.
Terror reminds me of ghosts.
Terror smells of burnt food, like a fire.

Bethany Vinton (10)
Mortimer St Mary's School, Reading

What Is Sadness?

Sadness is blue, like the cold winter's breeze.
It tastes like tears and broken.
A deafening boom like thunder and lightning enters your ears.
Sadness is like a crunchy soggy sandwich.
Sadness is blue, like the cold winter's breeze.
Sadness is a flood of tears.

Grace Sophia Rose Hewitt (10)
Mortimer St Mary's School, Reading

What Is Wonder?

Wonder is great, joyful, brilliant, amazing, cool, wow and happy.
It reminds me of a wonderful magical land and on
the magical land, there's wonderful colours, magic colours like pink,
yellow, orange, white, red, baby blue, green, blue, silver, gold
and purple.

Wonderful people are kind, happy, sharing, joyful, great
And they make the land happy and great.
Once again the day rises again to be a wonderful world.

Liberty Cairns (10)
Mortimer St Mary's School, Reading

What Is Sadness?

Sadness feels like a cold wind passing,
The sound of a drum that'll never stop lasting.
Sadness tastes like a fruit that is sour.
Sometimes I feel sadness for longer than an hour.

Sadness looks like a very dark night,
Sometimes dark is all that's in sight.
Sadness is the colour of dark blue,
Sometimes black reminds me of sadness too.

Laura Munson (10)
Mortimer St Mary's School, Reading

What Is Anger?

Anger is as fiery as a dragon.
Anger feels like flesh and bone.
Anger smells like blood pumping in frustration.
Anger reminds me of a fine knight.
Anger looks like a blood stone as a red dragon's being boiled.
Anger tastes like your brain posted on a stick
Anger is as red and black as Hell.

Jake McKerron (10)
Mortimer St Mary's School, Reading

Sadness

Sadness is grey, it tastes so emotional.
Sadness is grey, it feels dreadful.
Sadness is grey, it smells like old dust.
Sadness is grey, it sounds so dreary.
Sadness is the sad colour of grey.
Sadness is grey, it reminds you of lost ones.
Ones who are in pain and ones who are weak.
Sadness is grey, it looks so sad.

Charlotte Masters (10)
Mortimer St Mary's School, Reading

Joy

Joy tastes like a juicy red apple.
Joy looks like children and adults being happy and birds singing in the trees.
Joy feels like having a little spark inside yourself.
Joy smells like a rose in full blossom.
Joy sounds like children playing in the park.
Joy's colours are pink, yellow, blue and light green.
Joy reminds you of having fun when you were little.

Charley Tuttle (10)
Mortimer St Mary's School, Reading

What Is Wonder?

Wonder looks calm like a candle.
Wonder reminds people of what will be.
Wonder sounds like a calm blue sea.
Wonder tastes like a new chocolate bar.
Wonder smells like a new rose.
The colour is every colour.
It feels like you want to explore.

Amanda Brice (11)
Mortimer St Mary's School, Reading

What Is Love?

Love reminds me of your heart pumping fast.
Love looks sweet and kind.
Love tastes like cherry pie.
Love sounds like your heart beating.
Love smells like smelly roses.
Love is every colour in your mind.
And love feels soft, smooth, gentle and kind.

Tom Holmes (10)
Mortimer St Mary's School, Reading

What Is Pain?

Pain is as horrible as Brussels sprouts.
Pain smells of gone off mustard.
Pain reminds me of when my brother hits me.
Pain feels like rough sandpaper.
Pain looks like a massive bull coming at you.
Pain sounds like the worst song in the world.
Pain is as dark as the darkest red.

Archie Craissati (10)
Mortimer St Mary's School, Reading

Joy

Joy is the taste of a delicious cake.
Joy reminds me of my friends.
Joy looks like a child's smiling face.
Joy sounds like laughter and chuckles.
Joy is the colours of flowers.
Joy feels like a burst of colours.
Joy smells of lavender.

Shea Field (10)
Mortimer St Mary's School, Reading

Fun

Fun is yellow, hearing kids play in the park on a nice sunny day.
Fun is pink, like the lovely smell of a rose.
Fun is blue, like a river flowing by in the sunlight.
Fun is red, like a really hot day, having a picnic in the park.
Fun is purple, like a bright violet in the green, deep grass.
Fun is orange and the summer is here with a bright blue sky.
Fun is light green, having a picnic at the weekend at the park.

Molly Palmer (10)
Mortimer St Mary's School, Reading

Terror

Terror is black, like a chilled new moon on a Hallowe'en night.
Terror is black, like a merciless hand of a witch touching your spine.
Terror is black, like a cruel screech of a bat-like bird.
Terror is black, like your darkest, deepest nightmare.
Terror is black, like the smell of foul blood.
Terror is black, like the inky darkness of a cave.
Terror is black, like the blood of a black widow spider.

Thomas Adye (10)
Mortimer St Mary's School, Reading

What Is Sadness?

Sadness smells damp and like when things are being burnt.
It tastes sour like a lemon on its own.
The colour is the darkest colour you can think of.
Your heart has been smashed into thousands of bits.
It feels cracked and crumbles in your hand
Wet and squashy, like when you've been crying.
That's what sadness feels like to me.

Isobel Bunt (10)
Mortimer St Mary's School, Reading

What Is Love?

Love is a gentle sound, like a harp
Love tastes like calmness
Love looks like smelly roses
Love feels like soft flowers
Love is red, like roses
Love smells of rosy perfume
Love reminds me of happy times.

Rachel Thurley (10)
Mortimer St Mary's School, Reading

What Is Pain?

Pain is a scream of a sound
Pain is two colours getting mixed
And going all wrong.
Pain tastes like a raw egg or a sour lemon.
Pain smells like carbon monoxide
Poisoning the atmosphere.
Pain feels like you've lost someone important.

Charlie Holmes (10)
Mortimer St Mary's School, Reading

What Is Fun?

Fun is as wild as your dreams
Tastes like chocolate ice cream
As warm as a Barbados' sea
The colour of autumn leaves
Fun looks like mushy mud
Smells like a Monday spud.
Feels like a lumpy bowl of porridge.

Georgia Batty (11)
Mortimer St Mary's School, Reading

Fun

Fun is like the blue sky with children playing happily.
Fun sounds like people laughing with joy.
Fun tastes like the pink sweets ready to eat.
Fun is the colour of green grass that happy people have fun on.
Fun reminds me of my fun friends playing with me.
Fun smells of delightful people enjoying themselves.

Bethan Douglas (10)
Mortimer St Mary's School, Reading

What Is Anger?

The colour of anger is red because people go bright red in their face.
Anger tastes sour and bitter,
Anger looks red and upset,
It smells horrible, just like gone-off meat,
It sounds as loud as an elephant trumpeting,
Anger reminds me of pain and hurt.

William Barclay Clark (10)
Mortimer St Mary's School, Reading

What Is Love?

Love sounds like a Bugatti Veyron racing down the road
Love sounds like the cheer of the crowd when a goal is scored.
Love is the red of a Ferrari Enzo.
Love is the yellow of happiness.
Love is all the colours.
Love feels like the sweet drive of a Lamborghini Gallardo.

Edward Port (10)
Mortimer St Mary's School, Reading

Anger

Anger is a fizzy feeling, rising and raging.
Anger is fiery, overpowering and strong.
Anger is a storm, deafeningly loud.
Anger is a hurricane, terrifying and great.
Anger is a powerful feeling, a great adrenaline rush.
Anger reminds you of pain, a rending feeling.

Alastair Lavery (11)
Mortimer St Mary's School, Reading

Love

Love is red, like a big heart
It smells like pips but taste like chips.
It looks like hearts all around you.
It feels tempting, but not frightening.
Sometimes my rabbit bites me but still loves me.

Joshua Titcombe (10)
Mortimer St Mary's School, Reading

What Is Love?

Love is like a single heartbeat
And is also so calm and gentle.
It tastes like a fresh new family
Love is relaxing sat by a nice
Orange and calm, warm, loving fire.

Tia-Louise Bartlett (10)
Mortimer St Mary's School, Reading

A List Of Small And Big Feelings

How happy -
When you find
An eggshell even
Though it's dirty.

How proud -
When you find
A long-lost toy
But it's all broken.

How proud -
When you
Make something
Even though it's
Sixteen and over and
You're not that age.

How silly -
When you do
Something really
Funny that you
Laugh for ages.

How proud -
When you spot
The Easter bunny.

How embarrassed -
When your guitar
Strings break on stage.

Mikey Squire (9)
Ninfield CE Primary School, Ninfield

What Makes Me Happy

How happy -
when you take
a first bite of pasta,
with melted cheese on top

How happy -
When you discover
a pound down the back
of the sofa

How happy -
When you wake
up and your garden is
covered in snow

How happy -
When you see
the horses in
the field playing

How happy -
When you sprint
and you hear the
wind whistle in your ear

How happy -
When you find out that
you can eat a sugary bun
without licking your lips.

Ellen Sheppard (9)
Ninfield CE Primary School, Ninfield

What Makes Me Happy

How happy -
When you take the
First bite of a creamy ice cream

How happy -
When you find a 2 pound coin
Behind the sofa.

How happy -
When you find out you've
Won Charlie Bear
In assembly.

How excited -
When it is the summer holidays!

How happy -
When you wake up
And Santa Claus has been.

Joe Creasey (9)
Ninfield CE Primary School, Ninfield

MPH Show

Next month is my birthday
And I'm going to see some cars
I'm going into London
To see three well good TV stars.

There will be a cool Ferrari
Somewhere in the place
And a flashing Lamborghini
Which should always win the race.

The show is called 'Miles Per Hour'
The cars go really fast
I can't wait to see Jeremy Clarkson
And the cool Stig can't come last!

Christopher Shankland (8)
Queen Anne Royal Free CE First School, Windsor

Guinea Pigs

G reat weather will cover their life
U nique, they truly are
I llusion you might have had
N ever would you find a boring guinea pig
E normous animals look hungry
A tiny animal with a big appetite

P eru . . . the home of guinea pigs
I ncredible animals they are
G reat animals they are
S nakes will eat them up.

Louis Gregory
Queen Anne Royal Free CE First School, Windsor

Quiet Sounds Of The Countryside

The whistling wind whispers through the trees
The rustling leaves fly down
The soft breeze carries the snow
Swooping owls catch their prey
The boat bobs silently on the winding rivers.
Twigs crack as the squirrels scuttle quietly
Cows chomp the grass endlessly.
The birds keep on chirping, spring is on the way.

Toby Loughran (8)
Queen Anne Royal Free CE First School, Windsor

My Dog

My dog is fat and smelly
He doesn't have a mat but he likes to watch the telly
He likes to play
In some kind of way
He hates to sleep
And he bleeps
He doesn't like the dark
But he loves to bark.

Premleen Kaur Virdi (8)
Queen Anne Royal Free CE First School, Windsor

The River

The river's a baby
Gurgling through the ground,
Trying to get up
And wander around.

The river's a child
A friendly one too,
Meeting up with others
As they grow up too.

The river's a teen,
Desperate to be seen,
Quickly gushing through the town
Where he's already been.

The river's a giant
Flowing gracefully through the city,
Going out to sea,
What a pity.

Luke Russell (10)
St David's Primary School, Moreton-in-Marsh

The Magic Of Smell

Such a smell I smelt:
Potatoes, creamy and distinguishing,
Wine, strong and rich,
I felt like a king must do, walking into a palace.
I felt ravenous at this smell
Such a smell I smelt.

Such a smell I smelt,
Petrol fumes dizzying my head.
Clouds of smoke and metalwork on car.
Nauseating and ill I felt,
It made me want to dance in fresh air,
Such a smell I smelt.

Such a smell I smelt,
Cooked apples, steamy and soft,
Cinnamon, spicy, sugar on apple strudel
Refreshing my head.
Such a smell I smelt.

Such a smell I smelt,
Warm winter fires,
Smoke enwrapping my hands
Melt-in-your-mouth marshmallows,
And burnt paper or wood,
Taking my worries out of my head.

Such a smell I smelt
Calm, still fir trees,
Freshly fallen snow with a crust of ice,
A sprinkling of salt and early morning footprints
In the snow cooling and frosty, tender on my nose
Such a smell I smelt.

Such a world comes in through your nose
And through your head,
One of the five senses, as important as the others.
Smell is a wonderful thing,
But also a dreadful
Such a world comes through.

Charlotte Grace Davis (9)
St David's Primary School, Moreton-in-Marsh

Poetry Explorers 2009 - The South & South East

The Brilliance Of Sounds I Hear Each Day

Such a sound I heard,
The deep thudding of a horse thundering across a field,
The sound made me full of anticipation and excitement,
Gradually starting to snort as he began to tire,
Such a sound I heard.

Such a sound I heard,
The muffled, deep wicker of a pony waiting to be fed,
As he grew impatient he kicked the door with a shrill clang,
The noise sent a sharp shiver down my spine,
Such a sound I heard.

Such a sound I heard,
The faint clip clop of a pony trotting down the road,
The noise made me feel calm and fully in harmony with my pony.

And then we were back at the yard,
I listened to the sound of my pony's teeth grinding together as he munched his food,
The sound made me cringe a little but it also made me feel warm and content,
Such a sound I heard.

Such a sound I heard,
The high buzz of the judge's bell as I entered the competition,
The sound filled my stomach with butterflies
and my pony tugged at the reins,
I heard my mum calling the test and was transported to a dressage world,
Such a sound I heard.

Such sounds I hear every day,
I love these sounds so very much,
And they are so very familiar to me,
They make me feel like dancing and jumping for joy,
Such sounds I hear every day.

Phoebe Peters (10)
St David's Primary School, Moreton-in-Marsh

The Sight Of A Late Summer Day

Such a sight I saw
The bright sun shining like a big ball of fire,
Its beams of light gleaming down on my tanned-skin face,
It makes me feel warm and delighted.
Such a sight I saw.

Such a sight I saw
The beautiful, colourful bird elegantly swooping down,
As he curiously looks for the right landing.
It makes me feel like flying and dancing.
Such an elegant sight I saw.

Such a sight I saw
Crawling and scattering minibeasts,
The moving of their many different colours, red, orange, green,
It makes me feel interested and alive
Such a wonderful sight I saw.

Such a sight I saw
The soft but rapid swaying and swooping of the trees.
It is wonderful when the bright green leaves come down.
It makes me feel wonderful and free.
Such a sight I saw!

Such a sight I saw
Glowing like the sun's reflection with a small curly stalk
Its petals look so silky, I want to feel them,
It makes me feel light and calm but also wild and glowing
Such a sight I saw.

Such a sight I could see on a late summer's day
The trees and birds that make me dance and sway.
It's nature around I see with my sight, makes me feel alive
And free with delight
Such a sight I could see on a late summer's day.

Lidie Considine (10)
St David's Primary School, Moreton-in-Marsh

Such A Sight I Saw

Such a sight
A lovely rose sitting in the garden.
The stem was a bright green,
And standing in the dug up mud
Such a rose I saw.

Such a sight
A giant red wood standing
With his mates
115 metres high
Such a red wood that I saw.

Such a sight
A thorn bush all prickly and short.
Beautiful flowers growing beside it
And outside a house
Such a thorn bush I saw.

Such a sight
A sunset on the beach
Big waves with the sun behind them
Kids splashing in the water
Such a sunset I saw.

Such a sight
A rainstorm crashing
On the ground,
People running to get shelter,
Such a rainstorm I saw.

Such a sight
A playground full of kids
Playing football or bull tag
Kids falling on the grass
Such a playground I saw.

Josh Lewis (9)
St David's Primary School, Moreton-in-Marsh

Such A Touch I Felt

Such a touch I felt
Fluffy and warm all up my face.
Comforting as my pet snuggled my lap
Such a touch I felt.

Such a touch on my head.
Soft and loving as I sank in the pillow.
Helping me go to sleep.
So soft, so warm.
Such a touch on my head.

Such a touch of warmth
As I snuggled up to my blanket.
On a cold winter's night
Such a touch of warmth.

Such a soft touch I felt
Cuddly and warm on a scary damp night
With my teddy in my arms I know I'm safe
Such a soft touch I felt.

Such a touch I felt
Hard and wet
As I fell on the stones
Hurt and in pain as I lay in the stones
Such a touch I felt.

Such a touch I felt
The bark of the trees.
Rough and scratchy.
Hurtful and wet.
Such a touch I felt.

Natasha Hanks (9)
St David's Primary School, Moreton-in-Marsh

Perfect!

Such a smooth feeling I felt,
The velvety muzzle of a snoozing horse,
He whickers gently causing my hand to vibrate,
It made me feel calm and happy
Such a smooth feeling I felt.

Such a steady feeling I felt.
Cantering through a dew-covered forest.
Branches brushed against me as my pony rode on.
Made me feel alone, complete.
Such a steady feeling I felt.

Such a rushed feeling I felt,
Speeding up on the track as we approached the jump.
He leapt and we soared over the jump,
My legs squeezing his soothingly warm body.
We'd won!
This made me feel fantastic, a champion!
Such a rushed feeling I felt.

Such a warm feeling I felt
As I ran my finger up his back and his crest.
A soft, silky mane cascading down his neck
Made me feel content, other worldly
Such a warm feeling I felt.

Such a feeling I felt
All of these things happen once a week, or once a month,
Or once a year.
Perfect!
Such a feeling I felt.

Rachel Silcock (10)
St David's Primary School, Moreton-in-Marsh

The Magic Of Sound

Such a sound I heard
A wolf howling gracefully at sunset,
It sounded like a well known tune,
It made me feel like sleeping
Such a sound I heard.

Such an unpleasant sound I heard
A car screeching round a bend.
Viciously bursting eardrums,
It made me feel deaf
Such an unpleasant sound I heard.

Such a relaxing sound I heard
A bird tweeting in the dead of night.
Sitting in a leafless tree
It made me feel happy
Such a relaxing sound I heard.

Such a horrible sound I heard
A train thundering through a station,
It was sounding like an out of tune guitar,
It made me feel like covering my ears
Such a horrible sound I heard.

Such a beautiful sound I heard
The sea washing up on the rocks
Swaying peacefully and calmly
It made me feel like dancing
Such a beautiful sound I heard.

Connor Moore (11)
St David's Primary School, Moreton-in-Marsh

What A Sound I Heard

Such a sound I heard:
A wolf howling in the gloomy night,
It stood tall and proud on the perch of a cliff,
It made me feel like I was lying on my bed.
Such a sound I heard.

Such a pestering sound I heard:
A bunch of seagulls cheeping wildly,
They swept past like the Red Arrows but deafening.
It made me feel like I was in a room full of speakers.
Such a pestering sound I heard.

Such a peaceful sound I heard:
The peaceful sound of the gentle wind
It calmly whistled through my ears
It felt like music in my ears
Such a peaceful sound I heard.

Such an annoying sound I heard:
The horrible sound of nails against a chalkboard
It screeched and squealed like a baby
It made me feel like I was in Hell
Such an annoying sound I heard.

Such a pleasant sound I heard:
A drop of rain hit the ground continuously
Drip, drop, drip, drop,
It made me feel like dancing
Such a pleasant sound I heard.

Colby Townley (10)
St David's Primary School, Moreton-in-Marsh

The Magic Of Smell

Such a smell I smelt.
Roses mixed with rare perfume.
It took me back to winter and
My home all covered in rose vines
Such a smell I smelt.

Such a smell I smelt,
Curry and fish mixed with a dustbin smell,
Smelly socks after hockey,
The smell of Mitzi after a bath
Such a smell I smelt.

Such a smell I smelt,
The smell of Christmas cake fills the house.
I feel calm and peaceful,
Such a smell I smelt.

Such a smell I smelt
Fumes of the bathroom after sisters have been in
Pizza wafting through the house,
White chocolate, Green and Blacks
Such a smell I smelt.

Such a smell I smelt
It makes me feel as relaxed as ice cream
Smells come from the Horse and Groom.
Chips coming from next door
Such a smell I smelt.

Charmian Monroe (9)
St David's Primary School, Moreton-in-Marsh

Poetry Explorers 2009 - The South & South East

So Many Things To Feel

Such a touch I felt
Furry fur on a cuddly soft bear
Full of warmth and love
Such a touch I felt.
Such a touch I felt
It was hard like the waves crashing
Against the rocks, seaweed!
Such a touch I felt.
Such a touch I felt
My head crushing against a warm silky duvet cover,
Warm on my feet.
Such a touch I felt.
Such a touch I felt
Smooth and newly layered snow,
As I crouched in the snow, my feet were frozen . . .
Such a soft feeling I felt
As I walked on soft soggy leaves,
Making me sleepy as I fell on them.
Such a soggy feeling I felt.
Such a soft feeling I felt
As the scorching sun burnt my back
Such a warm feeling I felt.
Such a feeling I felt
As the world came to wonder
So many feelings I've felt.

Katie Griffin (9)
St David's Primary School, Moreton-in-Marsh

The River

A river is a sculptor, vigorously carving its endless way through a cold damp countryside.
The river is a vandal, demolishing every living thing in its pathway.
A river is a master, guarding and commanding its track.
A musician performing a melody over rocks and swaying weed.

Thomas Shurmer (10)
St David's Primary School, Moreton-in-Marsh

The River

The river is a farmer
Rounds up weeds.
As it splashes its way through
Just looking as if it was planting seeds

The river is a sculptor.
As it was magic in the landscape.
It carves its way through by beautiful twists.
Oh I love the peaceful movement.

The river is a musician.
It plays its instrument very beautifully
Echoes every drop of melody rain
As it twists and turns gracefully.

The river is a hunter
It hunts glittery frantic fish
As it splashes viciously through rocks.
But it does carry on.

Amelia Jasinski (9)
St David's Primary School, Moreton-in-Marsh

Autumn

The autumn wind with frosted breath,
The freezing sheet of ice covering the land.
With acorns falling like bombs,
As the leaves dance down like the gentle music they are.
The trees as giants of Earth, standing tall, swaying with each other.

The mice have packed up, escaping the uncertain weather,
While the rabbits are playing freely to be hunted.
Pheasant feathers fly to the ground,
With Christmas coming the food needs to be found.
Autumn is over,
Up goes the cheer,
Christmas is now very near.

Henry Oughton (10)
St David's Primary School, Moreton-in-Marsh

The River

The river is an actor,
Dramatising its voyage to the ravenous sea

The river is a sprinter,
Darting down the mountainside,
Dodging its way around obstacles.

The river is a sculptor,
It beautifies the countryside with majestic shapes and patterns.

The river is a musician,
It plays a mystical melody as it breezes through the rocks.

The river is a vandal,
Bombarding its way through the jagged valley.

The river is a rambler,
It is a gypsy gushing and weaving through the glistening plants.

Thomas Chapman (10)
St David's Primary School, Moreton-in-Marsh

The River

The river is a dancer
It twists and turns and meanders,
Calmly along the daylight.
Jumping up and down until the end of moonlight.

The river is a hunter,
It fights and fights with all its might,
Gushing through the water, forcing its way
Through everything.

The river is a protector,
It bundles the fish round and round,
Making sounds of bubbling beneath the lake.

The river is a master, it goes on adventures towards
The sea, commanding plants slowly along the coast.

Monaswee Millward-Brookes (9)
St David's Primary School, Moreton-in-Marsh

The River

The river is a boxer,
It punches vigorously,
Through twigs and currents,
To hopefully fight its way to the sea.

The river's a hunter
It chases down the stream
It swallows stones and rocks
It's brutal and it's mean.

The river's a sculptor,
It skilfully shapes the sides,
Sculpting with the waves
Mysteriously glides.

The river's a dancer,
It happily twirls.
Happy as ever,
Calmly swirls.

Sophie Gould (10)
St David's Primary School, Moreton-in-Marsh

The River

The river is a hunter
Chasing rapidly downstream
Searching for prey;
Twigs and rocks.

The river is a boxer,
Punching rapidly downstream,
Making its way to the big sea.

The river is a sculptor,
Beautifying the landscape,
Downstream carving
And meandering carefully.

The river is a musician,
Playing peacefully as it
Carefully meanders through
The valley.

William Wall (10)
St David's Primary School, Moreton-in-Marsh

My Dog

Tail wagger
Ankle biter
High jumper
Loud growler
Fast eater
Fast runner
Loud snorer
Finger nipper
Toe licker
Cat chaser
Paper ripper
Good scratcher
Hair biter
Shoe nicker
Slow walker
Bike chaser
And scared of everything.

Callie Parker (8)
St Mary's CE Primary School, Welham Green

Disco Diva

If you want a disco diva.
You have to pull the lever.
Put your dancing shoes on.
And wait for the song.
Show your moves.
Get the grooves.
Disco ball.
Lights up the hall.
If you want to show.
Get down low.
Get the flow.
So everyone let's go.

Bryony Richardson (9)
St Mary's CE Primary School, Welham Green

The Rich And The Poor

The rich have all the money,
The poor have nothing,
They lay their head to sleep in the streets,
While the rich are on soft satin sheets.

P enniless with nothing to their names,
O nly themselves for company
O nly the streets for a home
R egrets so big, where did they go wrong?

R egrets, they have none
I gnorant to the poor and needy
C aring only for themselves,
H aving all the money but never spending it on others.

The rich and the poor
There is a difference.

Hannah Yvonne Newell (10)
St Mary's CE Primary School, Welham Green

West Ham United

W est Ham are great
E very time they're always on the go.
S o with the help of Robert Green we're going to win
T he Boleyn Ground is the best place ever.

H ow can I ever thank you West Ham?
A nd like my dreams
M any thanks to Robert Green.

U pson is number 15.
N oble scores once again!
I go with my dad.
T revor Brooking was Daddy's favourite player
E very match they're always on the go
D addy loves them too.

Dana Connell (8)
St Mary's CE Primary School, Welham Green

Dolphin Kennings

Tail flapper
Wave smasher
Playful swimmer
Diving teacher
Fish eater
Meat eater
Seagull hater
Great jumper
Sea lover
Ocean breather
Wave lover.

Connor MacKintosh (10)
St Mary's CE Primary School, Welham Green

Dolphin

A royal jumper
A good swimmer
A great flicker
The best diver
Perfect splasher
Lives in water
A brilliant feeder
A good eater
A hard listener
It flicks higher.

Montana Sutton (9)
St Mary's CE Primary School, Welham Green

Christmas

C hristmas crackers with prizes flying out.
H olly prickles, please don't touch.
R ipping presents as we go.
I t's time to put yours out.
S anta is coming soon.
T ime is running out, hurry and go to bed.
M any people getting ready for this day coming up.
A carrot ready for the reindeer.
S anta is coming very soon.

Megan Ann-Marie Davies (9)
St Mary's CE Primary School, Welham Green

The Sea

The sea is blue
And it glimmers too
Dolphins splash around
And make a crashing sound
Treasure beneath the sea
I'd like to find pearls for me
Mermaids are beautiful and pretty
They have their own under the sea city.

Darcie Richardson (9)
St Mary's CE Primary School, Welham Green

Rascal

(Dedicated to my bearded dragon who sadly died, 24/9/09)

R ascal was my little friend
A nd I loved him very much,
S ince he died and went to Heaven, I've
C ried and cried and cried.
A nd I will always love him, he'll
L ive forever in my heart.

Jessica Bliss (10)
St Mary's CE Primary School, Welham Green

New School

It's time to settle in,
Remember what class you're in,
You need to act cool,
In your new school,
The teachers might seem cruel,
If you don't follow their rules,
But once you've been there a couple of weeks,
You'll get used to all your seats.

Danielle Tibbitts (9)
St Mary's CE Primary School, Welham Green

Why I Like Frogs

F ast creatures,
R ed, green and yellow,
O dd jumpers.
G reat climbers.
S uper swimmers.

This is why I like frogs!

Matthew Swift (9)
St Mary's CE Primary School, Welham Green

My Friend Amy

A Ferrari at top speed,
A mysterious young girl,
As dazzling as anyone could be,
A helpful, polite person,
The funniest person in my class,
My best friend Amy.

Elle-May Axford (10)
St Mary's CE Primary School, Welham Green

Fantasy

Fairies, goblins, trolls and elves,
We all made them ourselves,
Live in the fantasy,
Live how you're meant to be,
Live in the fantasy with me.

Witches, wizards, magic cats,
They all wear those pointy hats.
Sacks and sacks of sparkly gold,
Lead to nights out in the cold.
Remember these tales until you're old.

Barking horses, talking dogs,
Evil villains that wear clogs.
Tall towers of the villain's home.
Deep down in the sea lays a magical comb.
Flying pigs that live in Rome.

Amy Louise Settle (9)
St Mary's CE Primary School, Welham Green

The Dolphins

I like to hear the dolphins splashing in the sea.
I like to see the beautiful dolphins swim along in the sea.
I like to feel the dolphin's smooth skin when
I ride on the dolphin's back!
I like the smell of the dolphins when I swim with them.

Megan Waller (9)
St Mary's CE Primary School, Welham Green

Cats

C uddly furry animals
A nd I love them most of all
T ogether we are a family
S o I love cats most of all.

Caitlin Horne (8)
St Mary's CE Primary School, Welham Green

I Will Put Into My Fishing Box . . .

My buttercup-yellow float that slowly drifts on the water's surface.
My heavy lead weight that will sink into the murky mud.
A razor-sharp hook that stabs the maggot to catch the fish.
Ugly slippery maggots that wriggle as you pick up your bait.
The screaming reel when the line whizzes as the flopping, flapping fish jumps and flips over.

Ross Dyer (10)
St Mary the Virgin CE Primary School, Hartfield

Blazing Hot Sun

Tingling, flaming, scorching heat
Scorch your red-hot feet
Bumbling, bopping
Skating heat
Sand rushing
Wind whistling
Smash, crash desert.

Lenny Munn (9)
St Mary the Virgin CE Primary School, Hartfield

The Magic Box
(Based on 'Magic Box' by Kit Wright)

I will put in the box . . .
A spiky conker waiting for an autumn day to turn beautiful, smooth and silky,
A red, shining, gleaming balloon that shivers in the dark
And a beautiful white horse that will take me everywhere I want.

I will put in the box . . .
A happy puppy that will cheer me up when I'm feeling sad,
A soaring golden eagle that will fly where no other bird would go
And a fountain pen that will help me on my poems, work and writing.

I will put in the box . . .
A little goldfish that will help me forget about all the bad things that happen,
A witch's broomstick to fly me out in the night to see the world
And the smell of a fresh rose from the Queen's garden to freshen up my little box.

My box is fashioned from gleaming sand to a gold medal
With gleaming diamonds on the lid and big surprises in the corners.
The hinges are made from stone-hard steel
So it won't snap my magic little box.

Amelia McElligott (10)
St Mary the Virgin CE Primary School, Hartfield

Deadly Animals

The scorpion is like a ninja hiding in the darkness,
You will never know when it might strike,
When it strikes you may be close to death or not.

The tarantula also silent and deadly, hiding under the rotten hollow trees.
This creature can be so deadly it can kill you in minutes.
Its hairy legs, different colours, black, orange and brown.

Something is lurking in the murky brown and green swamp.
People don't even go near the swamp because this animal is so deadly
It can swallow a human whole.
As it slides into the water, it vigorously splashes in the swamp.
In the murky brown and green swamp is a dark green spiky crocodile.

Something is hiding in the leaves on the humid forest floor.
It slithers and slides on the forest floor,
It's so camouflaged in the leaves that you can hardly see it.
So that's why this creature is so deadly.
So what is hiding on the forest floor?
A big-headed king cobra.

Cameron Follows (10)
St Mary the Virgin CE Primary School, Hartfield

I Will Put In My Soup . . .
(Inspired by 'Magic Box' by Kit Wright)

I will put in my soup . . .
The brain of a bloodthirsty bear
The juice of a fresh flower from a Jubjub tree
Then the smell of freshly cut grass.

I will put in my soup . . .
The sweat of a professional diver
And the tongue of a blobber
Then the ink of a royal quill.

I will stir my soup with . . .
The spine of a clumsy gymnast
Playing at Wembley Stadium
And the shell of a Glob Glob egg.

I will eat my soup
On the massive moon, sharing it with the mysterious man on the moon.
Glug, glug.
As my soup trickles down my throat I find myself at home
Sitting in bed with my soup in my hands.

Mollie Kent (10)
St Mary the Virgin CE Primary School, Hartfield

The Creature

Deep down in the murky pond,
The creature is lurking,
With scales like wire and curls all blond,
The ghastly creature is born.

It fights its way up through the mud
Then glides gracefully through the water,
The sun catches its blood-red fangs,
Its deadly quest is slaughter.

Delicate wings touch the air as the creature starts to take flight,
It lets out a deadly screech and fills the world with fright.

It flies through the air quickly
And knocks down everything in its path,
The goo falling from it is sickly.
It bites animals down in half.

How the world is ruined,
Nothing is alive,
Apart from the terrible creature,
Which will survive.

Lauren Millie Oliver (11)
St Mary the Virgin CE Primary School, Hartfield

White Woman

A woman dressed in white stepped out onto her balcony,
Her silk dress billowing in the mid-summer night air.
The moon sent shadows over the wet garden
And made her long hair look like golden thread fit for a king.
Bitter tears filled her eyes and then leaked over and fell down her cheek,
She looked up at the moon and at the way it made everything glow silver.
The grass glistened with droplets of dew
And the air was filled with the sweet smell of honeysuckle.
The tree's branches moved with the wind making them look like arms reaching out to grab her
And her sobs were drowned out by the crickets calling calmly to the moon.
Around her white neck, a row of sparkling white pearls she wore
And a dozen silver bangles jingled up and down her arms
And her bare feet made no sound on the stone floor.
A woman dressed in white stepped out onto her balcony,
Her white dress billowing in the mid-summer night air.

Elizabeth Anne Townsend (10)
St Mary the Virgin CE Primary School, Hartfield

Hot, Hot Desert

The sun is blazing hot today.
It feels like I am walking through flames.
The sand is steaming beneath my feet.
I wish I was at home.

Amelia Rose Cranham (9)
St Mary the Virgin CE Primary School, Hartfield

My Magic Box
(Based on 'Magic Box' by Kit Wright)

I will put in my magic box . . .
A thin piece of string dipped into the thick white snow.
A spider's web covered in magical dew.
A falling silver star tumbling down from the sky as it strikes midnight.

I will put in my magic box . . .
The last corn standing on a winter's night.
The first shoot of a rose at the start of spring.
Little green shoots of grass appearing from the freezing ground.

I will put in my magic box . . .
The bright gold sun waking up after a long winter's sleep.
The little yellow chicks growing into big feathery chickens.
The splashing of children jumping into the crystal-blue water.

My magic box has nature of all the times of the year in it from winter to spring to summer.

My magic box is covered in white snow, red petals and golden sun.

Maia Wellbelove (10)
St Mary the Virgin CE Primary School, Hartfield

Friendship

F riends are for helping when you're stuck
R oaming through the salty seas together, never letting go
I have fights with them shouting and screaming, we always make up
E ver-going friendship that will never end
N umber and letter games we will play
D ancing and singing, we do that together too
S tanding steadily sad and alone which will never do
H appily hand-holding as we walk
I n our friendship worlds
P ushing and pulling will do us no harm, if we're together we'll make it through.

Megan Maria Maunsell (10)
St Mary the Virgin CE Primary School, Hartfield

Food To Eat

I will put in my mouth . . .
A delicious chocolate cake with butterscotch sauce on top.
It's like a lollipop and it tastes so nice.
I like it, and you should too because it's very chocolatey.

I will put in my mouth . . .
A delightful fruit salad, with different kinds of fruit.
It has a pineapple in it, it's as sweet as candyfloss.
It is so enjoyable because of all the different kinds.

I will put in my mouth . . .
A roast dinner with loads of things on my plate.
It's so nice that I could eat another small plate again.
It's like nothing you have had before.

I will put in my mouth . . .
An ice cream, like an exotic toffee twist.
It's so nice that I could eat it forever.
I never dreamed to have the toffee twist.

Marcus Goldsmith (10)
St Mary the Virgin CE Primary School, Hartfield

I Will Put In My Box . . .
(Based on 'Magic Box' by Kit Wright)

I will put in my box . . .
A whole load of screaming jelly babies screaming for their lives.
A triple ice cream drizzled with vanilla and toffee cream.

I will put in my box . . .
A haunted prison with the dead spirits tugging at the chains as the vicious dogs kill them.
The screams of the dead.

I will put in my box . . .
A zillion stars in the sky flickering like the gold
And the sun and the moon.

Peter Ottman (10)
St Mary the Virgin CE Primary School, Hartfield

The Dark, Daring Desert

I am a mouth-watering desert,
A bad desert who can make you curse until you reach the treasure.

I have three diamonds hidden in me.
You can try to get them if you dare.
People have tried for a hundred years.
Their bones are buried deep.

The blazing heat burns you.
You will not make it through me.

Two doors to choose from.
One leads to your home,
The other to the daring diamond challenge.

My challenges are hard.
Most people have failed,
What will your choice be?

In the dark, dangerous desert.

Kia Ivars (8)
St Mary the Virgin CE Primary School, Hartfield

The Fire King

He would send out boiling heat waves all over the desert
And boil the sand that would lie underneath your feet
Bubbling, scorching fire
Burning sun that burnt anything that would disturb its habitat
Floor cracking, skin peeling, black sky melting,
Rain boiling sand.

He wouldn't stop the heat waves until his challengers would surrender.
He will fight and fight and fight until the sun goes down
And he's finished his shift but tries to carry on.

I introduce you to the desert
Also nicknamed, the Fire King.

Laura Johnson (9)
St Mary the Virgin CE Primary School, Hartfield

Sad Frog

A slimy frog lived in a swamp
Croaking all night.
It was dark.
The frog was lost
Jumping high and low.

The frog's home had gone now.
Frog was sad.
He saw another frog,
She was green like a leaf in the night.
They searched for a home,
It was sticky and smelly
So they did not like it.

They built a new house.
Jumped up high
Shouting, 'Calloo callay.'
They were happy in the sun.

Katelyn Sleet (10)
St Mary the Virgin CE Primary School, Hartfield

The Magic Box
(Based on 'Magic Box' by Kit Wright)

I will put in my box . . .
A star from the night sky,
A second sun
And the horn from a unicorn.

I will put in my box . . .
A ninja dressed in black, ready to attack,
A cheetah sprinting by like a spaceship at lift-off.

I will put in my box . . .
A pair of arms grasping at a chocolate-brown chainsaw
And a slimy, silver saucepan full of ocean-blue water.

Robert Matthew Howey (10)
St Mary the Virgin CE Primary School, Hartfield

I Will Put In My Blender . . .
(Inspired by 'Magic Box' by Kit Wright)

I will put in my blender . . .
A king-size cheesecake with extra cream fit for a king.
A newborn beaver with a chainsaw destroying everything it sees
And a talking Jabberwocky babbling on, driving people crazy.

I will put in my blender . . .
A very tired person who falls asleep on the ceiling
And a fat policeman eating a doughnut
And a violin with ears that plays music to itself.

I will put in my blender . . .
An alien that sings 'Amazing Grace' backwards in Spanish while riding the unicycle
And some ice cream that isn't edible when it's cold
And finally a basketball that was once president
And now I shall enjoy this fine refreshment . . . *bluurrr.*

Zeke Jenkins (10)
St Mary the Virgin CE Primary School, Hartfield

The Magic Box
(Based on 'Magic Box' by Kit Wright)

I will put in the box . . .
A huge bag full of delicious mallows
A chocolatey creamy cake
And a hot, hot pizza like flaming fire.

I will put in the box . . .
A shiny, brand new phone
My bright green iPod
And my musical 'Jonas Brothers' CD.

I will put in the box . . .
My funky Animal Instinct T-shirt
My paint-splattered shoes, like I have just painted them
And my favourite, trendy Pineapple skirt.

Kirstie Sherry (10)
St Mary the Virgin CE Primary School, Hartfield

The Piddlenitch And The Knight

Knight Funny-Hat was sent to kill the piddlenitch
But the piddlenitch was very hard to find
Because it lived in Tumble Tree Forest,
But it was the only thing on his mind.

'The time has come!' said the knight,
To his army of three.
'We can't let this monster rampage like a running, red-eyed, rotting bull!'
'Why can't we just leave it be?'

'Because it's killed lots of people!' shouted Knight Funny Hat.
'No it has not,' said the knight and he pushed Funny Hat.
Funny Hat stumbled and fell out of the open window
And that was that.
He was dead.

Maddie Noddings (10)
St Mary the Virgin CE Primary School, Hartfield

I Will Put Into My Shed . . .
(Inspired by 'Magic Box' by Kit Wright)

I will put into my shed . . .
A football from the Chelsea manager which glistens in the sky
And a proper professional pump.

I will put into my shed . . .
A brilliant bullet bike that will ride faster than ever,
With seven speed gears.

I will put into my shed . . .
A football stadium (the biggest in the world)
And a cricket stadium that will have the largest amount of seats.

I will put into my shed . . .
A chainsaw still running
And a strimmer to stop the grass growing longer.

Sam Rickets (10)
St Mary the Virgin CE Primary School, Hartfield

Dreams

In my dream was . . .
A playful puppy with a ball
A brave knight on a white horse
And an old willow tree shining in the sun as it leaned over a peaceful stream.

In my dream was . . .
A werewolf howling at the moon,
The smell of a rose in the middle of a dark wood
And the creamy taste of a chocolate chip cake.

In my dream was . . .
A resting kitten asleep in a basket,
A beautiful white wedding when the leaves were falling
And the first smile of a small baby.

Alice Willemina Moore (10)
St Mary the Virgin CE Primary School, Hartfield

Monster Of The Drain

Something was lurking underneath the floorboards.
It was in the basement.
Bang! Crash! Then all was still.
I saw a mysterious figure.
I went past the front door and the window sill.
I rushed down to the basement
And it went through the walls.
It chased me round and round the room
And hit me with footballs.
It chased me up the stairs and it chased me in the garden
And I squashed it down the drain, where it really belongs . . .

Ben Lyons (9)
St Pancras Catholic Primary School, Lewes

My Birthday

I just can't wait, I really can't wait for my birthday
I get to see my really best mates for my birthday

Everyone is in a good mood for my birthday
We have some lovely food for my birthday

We have sausages in a bun for my birthday
The games are very fun for my birthday

I love my birthday, it is so great
I really, really cannot wait for my birthday.

Rosie Hastings (8)
St Pancras Catholic Primary School, Lewes

Flowers!

Flowers are all different shapes
And sizes no matter what you do.
Flowers are all different colours,
Red and blue flowers.
When the wind comes, the flowers swish and swash.
Flowers grow and grow before you can say go and no.
Flowers are nature, they are such a good thing.
Flowers are such a beautiful thing,
I don't know what I would do without them.

Jodie Watson (9)
St Pancras Catholic Primary School, Lewes

The Wind

The wind is as cold as a freezer.
The wind is as hot as a volcano.
The wind is as slow as a snail.
The wind is as invisible as a spy.
The wind is as fast as a cheetah.
The wind is as strong as a wrestler.

Rhiannon Davies (9)
St Pancras Catholic Primary School, Lewes

My Mad Brother

I was sitting at the table with nothing to do
When my little baby brother came up to me
Then he chased me out the room
With a zoom
Then hit me with a spoon
Then I had an idea
And gave him some beer.

Oliver Willett (8)
St Pancras Catholic Primary School, Lewes

Copper Becomes A Star

He was a puppy who I found in a wild land.
He was as pretty as a diamond.
He was as soft as a fluffy cat.
He was as cute as a newborn puppy.
His eyes were as blue as the sky.

Chelsea King (9)
St Pancras Catholic Primary School, Lewes

Mystery

I'm
Gliding like a bird
See me high in the sky
White as white can be
Take you places you have not been
If you want, you can have a pie
You can also do the crossword
I fly in the sky
And live in a port
And I import
Lots of goods
I am sometimes made of wood.

Henry Elsey (10)
Sapperton CE Primary School, Cirencester

What Am I?

I am
A rectangle
And I come in different colours.
I can connect to people
And have a touch screen with a pen.
I am powered by battery
And my head is a jumble of games.

What am I?

Ismé Mason (9)
Sapperton CE Primary School, Cirencester

What Am I?

I am a square box
That moves about
Non-stop images
I can shout
I can guide you to anything
Make you cry
But if I go fuzzy
Please stand by!

Erin Grady (11)
Sapperton CE Primary School, Cirencester

What Am I?

I am
A little friend who lives in a box.
I eat your files to keep them safe.
I am square and multicoloured.
I am used as a rubbish bin
And I shoot out thin white strips,
To keep my details safe from naughty, naughty culprits.

Ewan Crowden (10)
Sapperton CE Primary School, Cirencester

My Family Poem

I have a little brother, I'll start with him:
Joseph's his name, full of sin,
He will either make you mad . . .
Or make you grin.

There's another one called Tommy -
This one ain't so funny!
Cute as they come
But will steal all ya money.

Then there's Mum -
She's one for a laugh.
If she ain't in bed
She's in the bath!
Netball mad,
Always cutting hair -
Look what she's done to my fringe!
This just isn't fair!

Then we move on to my stepdad,
Stomping and shouting . . .
I think he's mad!
Will someone tell him to stop that racket!
He'll be in a straightjacket.

We have two dogs and a two bedroom home,
I want my own room!
'Someone give me a loan!'

Good times and bad times,
Arguments and sulks,
We are all so happy -
Despite our many faults.

Chloe Mullen (9)
Someries Junior School, Luton

Me

The writer of this poem
Has a very funny name,
Don't look at me!
I'm not the one to blame.
My hair is short,
My legs are too.
Just like my mum's,
My eyes are blue.
I have a sister,
She's a bit of a nut,
She is very annoying
And she moans a lot.
My dog is called Barney,
He likes to play
And he loves the walks
He gets every day.
Every weekend I go see my dad,
He lives in Milton Keynes
And he's absolutely mad!
My stepdad is cool,
My stepmum is too.
Enough about me,
How about you?

Kailan Derrick Pare (9)
Someries Junior School, Luton

Mum

My mum is full of surprises, which is why I get prizes.
If I fell in a puddle she would pick me up and give me a cuddle.
Her affection, independence and determination give me so much knowledge and confidence.
She is a beautiful emerald, which shines the brightest I have ever seen!
I love her so much because she's my mum.

Inayah Inam (9)
Someries Junior School, Luton

Autumn

Autumn, autumn,
Falling leaves:
Red, yellow and green.
Autumn, autumn,
Colder weather:
Chilly and damp.
Autumn, autumn,
Flowers dying -
Planting bulbs.
Autumn, autumn,
Bonfires burning and
Fireworks sparkling.
Autumn, autumn,
Squirrels hunting -
Nuts for lunch.
Autumn, autumn,
Darker nights and
Shorter days.
Autumn, autumn.

Andrew Hughes (9)
Someries Junior School, Luton

Firework Night

Bang! Bang! go the fireworks, 12 o'clock at night,
They are all pretty colours lighting up the sky.
Spark! goes a sparkler, sparkling in your hands -
Wave it up and down, wave it round and round.
Light up the rocket, watch it go -
It goes up in the sky and you wonder where it goes.
Sit around the bonfire, watching the fireworks go -
You see them go up into a sparkly glow.
Now the night is ending, you watch the fire glow,
We quietly go upstairs and watch out the window.
As the night sky finally glows.

Paige Wykes (9)
Someries Junior School, Luton

Butterflies

Beautiful butterfly of many colours
Flapping your delicate wings,
Quickly moving around the flowers
Gathering your nectar to eat.

Many different colours you are:
Reds, blues, yellows and white.
Both wings exactly the same -
Like a painting we could make.

Gracefully you fill the sky,
Gently moving around,
Having to be careful
In case predators are around.

Laying your eggs under the leaf
Waiting for them to hatch,
The small caterpillars go crawling,
Eventually sleeping until they become a butterfly.

Morgan Ella Lougher (9)
Someries Junior School, Luton

Rabbits

I like to keep rabbits as pets
And if you are caring and kind
They won't have to visit the vets.
Sometimes they're hard to choose
When you're looking to purchase a pet
It's better to keep them in twos.

You give them new food each day
To keep them healthy and strong,
You set a fresh layer of hay,
Give them lots of love and care.
I love them so much
But make sure everyone gets one to share.

Natasha Bonner (9)
Someries Junior School, Luton

My Pet Fish

Brian is always happy to see me
When I come home from class
He swims around in circles
And bumps into the glass.

Brian is always hungry
When I come home from school
I open up his food pot
And try to make him drool.

Brian is my best friend
I like to watch him swim
He wiggles his fins at me
With a little grin.

Sometimes Brian is lonely
When I'm at school all day
Maybe I'll buy him a little mate
A clownfish called Nemo made from clay.

Lauren Dilley (9)
Someries Junior School, Luton

Hallowe'en

Hallowe'en is here:
Time for witches, ghosts and vampires.
It's a party - a Hallowe'en party.
Lots of cakes and snakes,
Mummy faces here and there,
I swear that's the bogeyman over there!
Pumpkins are alight.
Watching the witches making frights.
Everyone come here,
The fireworks are over there!
Time to go -
Scare well!

Sarah Rigby (9)
Someries Junior School, Luton

School's Boring

School's very boring, I have to do it all day.
I would rather be at home and go on my PlayStation and play.
Maths and literacy are always first,
Numbers and words just give me thirst
To take a break and have some fun
And go outside so I'm not so glum.

After lunch, geography and history,
I have to research countries and learn about the past,
But I prefer the future.
Next is RE and PE,
I have to research religious relations,
PE is not so bad but I have to run really fast.

All the subjects get on my nerves,
But when it's home time that's just fine.
On Friday I stay for football at school
And that's really quite cool.

Ethan Paul Cox (9)
Someries Junior School, Luton

My Nan

She's quite wrinkly but still very pretty,
She's got brown eyes and wears glasses,
She's quite short and old but wears nice clothes,
She's got a red car and works in a chemist,
She loves crossword puzzles,
She's got a cat and a beautiful garden,
She makes me roast dinners, I love her cooking,
I like doing jigsaw puzzles with my nan,
She spoils me with cuddles and kisses,
She smells like perfume, she's soft and gentle,
I like to sleep at my nan's, it's comfy and cosy,
She may be clumsy but she's still very funny,
I know she loves me and she knows I love her.

Jake Simpkins (9)
Someries Junior School, Luton

Young Writers

Hallowe'en

Hallowe'en, Hallowe'en
Where have you been?
What have you seen?

The witches fly
High in the sky,
A black cat
Sitting on someone's doormat.

I don't want to go out in this weather,
My bag is as light as a feather.
It is so cold,
The witch is so old,
She is all green
And so, so mean!
That witch broke my pumpkin,
I snapped her broom,
I hope I don't see her any day soon!

Leah Irvine (10)
Someries Junior School, Luton

My Room

My room is such a mess.
I can't find my clothes when I dress.
I found socks in my bed
And pants on my head.

There's toys on my floor.
I can't open my door.
Tidying up is such a chore.
My brother and I would much rather explore.

I haven't got any space.
I can't find my shoelace.
I'd better tidy my room
And then my mum will be over the moon.

Zack Boutwood (9)
Someries Junior School, Luton

Spring, Summer, Autumn, Winter

In spring the flowers come out
Daffodils and tulips begin to sprout.
Trees and plants start to grow leaves -
You can even hear the humming of bees.
In the summer the sun shines hot -
It's nice to relax with an ice cream pot.
People on holiday are having fun,
Running around in the sun.
In the autumn the leaves start to fall,
Covering the ground in piles so tall:
Oranges, browns, yellows and greens
Making the most colourful blanket ever seen.
In the winter the snow comes down
Making me shiver and covering the town.
Snowmen and snowballs all over the place
Lots of kids are playing chase.

Luke Cresswell (9)
Someries Junior School, Luton

Football

There goes the alarm,
Not much of a charm,
When you're tired
And not feeling wired
Then you realise
And let out cries,
It's Saturday - hooray!
Time to play football with the team,
I score a goal and let out a scream,
It's 2000-0 and we're going to win,
One of their players is angry and jumps in the bin,
Then it's all over and we get in the car,
With a shiny trophy that shows we are the best by far.
Yeah!

Louie Teakle (9)
Someries Junior School, Luton

My Brother Joseph

I like him,
He's my little brother.
I like watching TV with him.
Playing games we make up:
I eat with my little mouth
And people in my family.

I race to the car with him every day,
I want to win always at everything,
So does he.

We have arguments sometimes
And I get cross,
But when I have my turn
I get happy again
Because Joseph is my brother.

Benjamin Morrison (9)
Someries Junior School, Luton

My Brother

I hate my brother, he is so, so mean,
He never lets me play on his Xbox machine.
He stays in his room and shouts, 'Go away,'
I only want him to come out and play.

He plays on his iPod all day long
And on MSN,
I think it's just wrong.
He should be outside playing football with me,
I'm his little brother, why can't he see?

I'm so sad and lonely, all on my own,
But I do love my brother; I'm just having a moan.

Oliver Gazeley (9)
Someries Junior School, Luton

Autumn Time

Autumn time has come again,
Cold, freezing and lots of rain.
Beautiful coloured leaves fall to the ground,
Listen to the breeze,
Blowing through the trees.

Squirrels are storing up their food,
The children are playing in the wood,
All wrapped up in scarves, gloves and hats.
I'm glad that autumn came,
But sadly it has got to go again.

Kimberley Piper (10)
Someries Junior School, Luton

Flowers

Flowers red,
Flowers blue,
Flowers make me think of you.

Flowers yellow,
Flowers pink,
When the wind blows, the flowers wink.

Flowers purple,
Flowers white,
Flowers in a garden, what a sight!

Olivia Victoria Pearce (9)
Someries Junior School, Luton

Now That My Grandma Is Gone

A shooting star came from Heaven, the night my grandma died.
It wrapped her up in sparkles and took her pain away.
It packed away her feelings, her happiness and joy.
It also took her memories of family and friends.
It wrapped them up together and blew them far away from me.

I really love my grandma, her smile brightened up my day.
Her face always shone like sunshine, with its golden rays.
I never saw this star again to be really true,
But the only thing I know is that I love my grandma too.

Evie Watts (9)
Someries Junior School, Luton

Nightmare Park

I went to the park,
It was very dark.
All of a sudden I heard a dog bark,
Then I heard an owl hoot
And it swooped down to catch a mouse.
I really wished I was back in my house,
I started to scream!
Then I woke up, it was a dream!

Jack Parrott (9)
Someries Junior School, Luton

Waking Up

The alarm clock goes off in the morning
And I wake up yawning,
Out of my bed I jump
And fall on the floor with a thump,
Down the stairs I run,
To have my breakfast, oh what fun.

Ben Pennifold (9)
Someries Junior School, Luton

Ill

I'm feeling very ill
And I have to take a pill
And I've got a really bad chill.

I ran down a hill
And I met a really lovely man called Will.

And I bought a big till
And on the way I spotted a windmill.

Paige Martin (9)
Someries Junior School, Luton

Poems

It takes some time
To make it rhyme
But it also needs grime
To make it in time.
Some people think it's lame
Because of its name.
What a shame because it can make your fame.

Emilio Vaughan Fletcher (9)
Someries Junior School, Luton

Football

I like football, it makes me feel alive.
Chasing the ball around the pitch, going in for the tackle as I slide.
As I score a goal the crowd start singing.
Could this be a chance of winning?
Time is ticking away, it is almost the end of play.
The whistle is about to blow, will we get another goal?
The game is done, I had lots of fun.

Adam Murgatroyd (9)
Someries Junior School, Luton

Untitled

The nights are drawing in.
That's why my mum keeps me in.
Through the window I watch the trees swaying,
Oh my god - it's now raining!
It's splashing on the floor,
Oh I wish I were outside playing football.

Johnathon Martin (9)
Someries Junior School, Luton

Swimming Lesson

Before I start swimming, I drink a cup of tea.
Swimming in the swimming pool is where I like to be.
I wear my underwater goggles so that I can see.
I won a swimming competition for my cub group,
It made me as happy as can be.
Swimming tires me out, it's time to go home for my tea.

Jack Rawlings (9)
Someries Junior School, Luton

There Is A Rainbow In The Sky

Here is a rainbow up in the clear blue sky,
Colourful and shiny just like you.
The clouds come in pure and clean.
There is a rainbow in the sky,
As you move slowly through the sky you shine so bright like a star.
There is a rainbow in the sky.
As you fade away all colourful and bright you will still be the same.
There is a rainbow in the sky
And will come out tomorrow so keep waiting.
So keep looking out for the glorious, shiny and colourful rainbow.

Rajdeep Kaur Chungh (10)
Tanners Brook Junior School, Southampton

Seasons

Summertime is my favourite, I get a big holiday,
Another reason for this is it happens to be my birthday!
I visit my dad and have a family tea
And then I get lots of pressies just for me!

Autumn is another, you get to jump in leaves,
Leaves are all around you, it is all you need.
Thank goodness the days are shorter,
It's time for me to sleep!

Winter is amazing, you get to play in snow,
Light up the tree and see Rudolph glow.
Share all your presents, have a family tea,
Don't forget to leave a present for me!

Flowers start to bloom, animals are born,
Children start to play, farmers grow their corn.
Frogs hop along, ribbet-ribbet hey!
This is what happens in spring today!

Faye Draper (10)
Tanners Brook Junior School, Southampton

Moonlight Poem

M oonlight shining
O utside in the garden
O wls howling
N othing is going on
L ights are off
I n the reflection of the
G lassy water
H ouse is gleaming
T ranquil and peaceful.

Nikita Adams (8)
Tanners Brook Junior School, Southampton

Sand, Sand

Sand, sand, everywhere
Between my toes and in my hair
Sand, sand, lots of fun
Every day for everyone
See seawater in front of me
But not a drop to drink
I can see an ice cream van
My favourite lolly's pink.

Taylor Robyn Murphy (9)
Tanners Brook Junior School, Southampton

Haunted House

H aunted with not a ghost to be seen
A nd a deserted hallway with vampire paintings.
U nique long table with lovely food awaiting you.
N othing to be heard from the horrible graveyard.
T empting to touch but mustn't.
E xciting secret passages to explore.
D ead bodies awaken. Argh!

Daniel Hallett (8)
Tanners Brook Junior School, Southampton

Boys!

Boys, boys, I hate boys
Making lots and lots of noise.
Boys, boys everywhere,
Picking noses, pulling hair.
Boys, boys, kick and punch,
Running riot, throwing lunch.
Boys should be abducted by aliens!

Eleanor Thomson (9)
Tanners Brook Junior School, Southampton

Beauty

B eautiful, stunning.
E xotic and peaceful.
A s the moon sparkles.
U nable to breathe because of its beauty.
T he ghostly trees swaying in the wind.
Y ou should really come and see it!

Mia Hulland-Banks (8)
Tanners Brook Junior School, Southampton

Night

N obody is there.
I n the gleaming moonlight.
G azing at the stars.
H igh in the sky the moon is so bright.
T his is a glamorous garden.

Emily Holmes (9)
Tanners Brook Junior School, Southampton

Night Poem

N othing is happening
I n the moonlight
G leaming in the pool
H ouse is quiet
T he moon is beautiful.

Laila Savage (8)
Tanners Brook Junior School, Southampton

Night Poem

N othing moving
I n the darkness
G littering moon
H igh reflection in the gigantic pool
T idy garden by the sea.

Shanice Christians (8)
Tanners Brook Junior School, Southampton

The Magic Box . . .
(Based on 'Magic Box' by Kit Wright)

In my box I will put . . .
The gleam of a diamond,
The first dance of a married couple,
The eyes of a loving mother.

I will put in my box . . .
The smell of a rose on Valentine's Day,
The trail of a school of fish,
The first kiss of a first lover.

I will put in my box . . .
The final command of a wise king,
The first flight of a duckling,
The sound of an aerial storm shooting down the track.

I will put in my box . . .
The smell of the English Channel,
The explosion of Mount Vesuvius.

My box is fashioned with pearl-white handles
And the sky as the lid.

I will live in my box,
Living a calm and happy life never growing old.
My box will never break as long as I am in the world I created.

Amanda Cooze (11)
Wexham Court Primary School, Slough

The Magic Box
(Based on 'Magic Box' by Kit Wright)

I will put in the box . . .
The roar of a desperate pterodactyl
The ballet steps of a bulldozer
A bite into the largest toffee apple.

I will put in the box . . .
A broomstick on a cowboy
A horse on a witch
The irresistible taste of a Krispy Kreme doughnut.

I will put in the box . . .
The hum from a speeding RAF jet
Never-ending music from the oldest steel pans
Sound of a pin dropping.

I will style my box of
Hinges of steel
Sides of copper
A lid of leather.

I shall swim in my box
In the calm, clear blue Atlantic
In the wavy swimming pool on the Titanic
In the Great Barrier Reef.

Ahmad Abu Mahfouz (11)
Wexham Court Primary School, Slough

She Is . . .

She is like the steady beat of a butterfly's wings.
She is like a giant tree reaching out towards the sky.
She is the light at the end of a tunnel.
She is the pillar that holds up my heart.
She is like a priceless stone gem stolen from the Sahara Desert.
She is the warm summer smile in a cold winter's night.
She is the strongest conker from the mightiest horse chestnut tree.

Samantha Kae Sedano Sotero (10)
Wexham Court Primary School, Slough

The Magic Box
(Based on 'Magic Box' by Kit Wright)

I will put in my box . . .
The coldest ice from the deepest pit
The bullet that ended World War II
The first tooth of a baby shark.

In my box I will put . . .
The clearest water from a diamond cave
The devastating punch of Mohammed Ali
The inspirational words of Martin Luther King
The first crumb of a chocolate cake.

In my box I will put . . .
The darkest curse of the White Witch
The brightest light from the dullest cave
The fiery meteor to end the dinosaurs
The vicious fangs of Count Dracula.

My box is fashioned with dark matter and platinum.
Its lid is made of gold bricks and iron cement.
Its lock is made with the howls of coyotes.
It is powered by the darkest secrets of heroes.

Bilal Ur-Rehman (10)
Wexham Court Primary School, Slough

She Is . . .

She is the light, brightening up the village.
She is the secret, ready to be opened.
She is the sound that is in my beating heart.
She is like a golden star shining brightly in my sky.
She is the blaze of warmth, cosying me up.
She is a flower with crystal-white petals.
She is a sparkle that lights in my eye.
She is the ancient melody, singing into my brain.
She is Cleopatra's lost tomb.

Sidra Chaudhry (10)
Wexham Court Primary School, Slough

The Magic Box
(Based on 'Magic Box' by Kit Wright)

I will put in the box . . .
The lovely sight of the Garden of Eden,
The heavenly taste of chocolate chip cookies,
The luxurious wind whistling my name.

I will put in the box . . .
The first lick of strawberry ice cream,
A scorching winter's day,
The smell of India as I take my first step.

I will put in the box . . .
A light in my heart guiding me towards the night,
A leaping dolphin dancing in the air
And the cheeks of a baby.

My box is made of . . .
Crystal clear icicles and purple silhouette felt,
Gold and silver diamonds shining beautifully
And one special photo of my mum.

Manraj Singh Tack (10)
Wexham Court Primary School, Slough

She Is . . .

She is the first and the last heartbeat of my life.
She is as elegant as a butterfly.
She is the soft cuddly duvet that I snuggle on to.
She is as clever as Albert Einstein.
She is as precious as the lost tomb of Cleopatra.
She is the full stop at the end of my sentence.
She is the hand that wrinkles with age.
She is the sun that covers my world.
She is the light at the end of the tunnel.
She is the missing piece of me.
She is the moat around my castle.

Rimsha Asad Satti (11)
Wexham Court Primary School, Slough

The Magic Box
(Based on 'Magic Box' by Kit Wright)

I will put in the box . . .
The last crumb of chocolate cake
A final roar of the last dinosaurs
The last breath of a dying man.

I will put in the box . . .
The first cry of a newborn baby
The clearest water from a diamond cave
The magic of a lucky leprechaun.

I will put in the box . . .
The ending bullet of World War II
The first touch of Heaven
And the last touch of Earth.

My box is fashioned by wool, wood and ice
There are secrets under each golden corner
And there are lots of magic things
There is a hidden button to activate the box.

Tawkir Kamali (10)
Wexham Court Primary School, Slough

Candle

The candle reminds me of Christmas,
Christmas with my family,
Its burning eye slowly melts its waxy body into a liquid puddle
And it makes me feel so sleepy
As it goes from tall to small and strong to weak.
It smells like vanilla ice cream.
Its ghostly smoke flies around the room as I dream,
Dream of a cake, a cake full of candles,
(1, 2, 3, 4, 5, 6, 7, 8, 9, 10 and 11 candles, all blown out).
I make my wish, I don't tell anyone as it's seven years' bad luck!

Bethany Money (10)
Wexham Court Primary School, Slough

She Is . . .

She is . . .
She is a cosy teddy that I hug at night.
She is the hot summer wind blowing across Hawaii.
She is all the colours of a bright rainbow.
She is the moat around my pretty castle.
She is a caring rabbit.
She is the sparkle in my brown eye.
She is a ruby rock that never smashes.
She is the precious hope in all the battles.
She is the candy that sweetens my heart.
She is the star that grants me my wishes.
She is the sun that never fades away.
She is the energy in the centre of the sun.
She is the flower opening on a hot summer's day.
She is one of the most precious things in my life.
She is the Great Wall of China wrapping her arms around me.
She is my first and last heartbeat.

Amrita Singh (10)
Wexham Court Primary School, Slough

Lent

This year I'm going to give up time,
Time to keep my bedroom clean,
Time to clean the kitchen floors of those pesky germs,
Time to sweep the fallen leaves beneath the willow trees,
Time to help when I feel like it,
Time to do my 11+ papers,
Time to leg it down for some cookies,
Time to carry heavy bags when my mum's come back from the shops,
Time to help my mum when she's feeling glum
And sit for a cup of juice,
Time to give others time
And in the end, some time for some fun (playing on the PS3).

Rameez Rashid (10)
Wexham Court Primary School, Slough

She Is . . .

She is the bright diamond which gives me inspiration,
She is one of the most precious things in my life,
She is the sun that never fades into the sky,
She is the sparkle in my eye,
She is the rock that never breaks,
She is all the colours of the rainbow,
She is the fossil in my heart,
She is the precious hope in battles,
She is the one and only person who will never cry, even through hard times,
She is the moat around my castle,
She is the angel in the sky,
She is a shiny seashell found in the mighty waters,
She is the flower opening on a hot summer's day,
She is the Great Wall of China wrapping her arms around me.

Kajol Jhandey (10)
Wexham Court Primary School, Slough

She Is . . .

She is as elegant as a butterfly.
She is as wise as an owl.
She is the sun that never fades.
She is always reminding me about summer.
She is as pretty as a beautiful flower.
She is a hot summer breeze.
She is a sparkle in my eye.
She is like the swish of a silk sari.
She is as clever as a calculator.
She is like the fossil in my heart.
She is like a cosy cup of tea.
She is as tough as a rock.
She is a pillar holding up my world.
She is the moat around my castle.
She is the key to my world.

Kiran Dhuga (10)
Wexham Court Primary School, Slough

The Magic Box
(Based on 'Magic Box' by Kit Wright)

I will put in the box . . .
The Starbucks' chocolate with whipped cream,
The cream from the Strawberry Dream chocolate,
The first lick of a chilling ice lolly on a scorching spring afternoon.

I will put in the magic box . . .
The luxurious bright red rose swaying gently in the wind,
The gigantic elephant stomping in the golden desert,
The first drop of rain in a drought.

I will put in the magic box . . .
The colours of the rainbow, exotic sunset fading away,
The upside-down rainbow,
The last day of romance on a hot summer's day - at midnight.

Sabrina Rukshar Mughal (11)
Wexham Court Primary School, Slough

The Magic Box
(Based on 'Magic Box' by Kit Wright)

I will put in the box . . .
The cream from the Strawberry Dream chocolate,
Starbuck's chocolate with whipped cream,
The gigantic elephant stomping in the golden desert.

I will put in the box . . .
A drop of rain in a drought,
An upside-down rainbow slowly fading away,
The colours of the whistling wind.

I will put in the box . . .
An enchanted unicorn dancing past our minds,
The last day of romance on a summer's day,
The light that leads us to salvation.

Husna Ahmed (10)
Wexham Court Primary School, Slough

She Is . . .

She is a cup of happiness overflowing,
She is the strongest rock at the bottom of the ocean,
She is an angel sent from Heaven,
She is the feeling of hope in my nightmare,
She is a gift that I can't wait to open,
She is the scent of fresh red roses,
She is the light at the end of a tunnel,
She is a bright summer's evening,
She is the sparkle in my eye,
She is as elegant as a pale white, mute swan,
She is a gentle lullaby sung to put a baby to sleep,
She is the largest diamond found in the smallest mine,
She is a book with a thousand pages.

Cerys Hanson (10)
Wexham Court Primary School, Slough

She Is . . .

She is a stubborn tree firmly holding down its roots,
She is a bright seven-coloured rainbow with an eighth colour I have no name for,
She is as beautiful as an emerald neatly cut into a million facets,
She is the bright light everyone waits for in a dark tunnel,
She is a flair of beautiful emotion,
She is the most beautiful dream anyone could imagine,
She is as hard as stone yet still as soft as a hamster,
She is the voice in your head telling you to do the right thing,
She is the infallible smile around us all,
She is a shoulder to cry on,
She is the secret diary you pour your heart and soul into,
She is the greatest person in my world!

Alina Parveen Malik (10)
Wexham Court Primary School, Slough

She Is . . .

She is the crystal in my eye.
She is like a ray of sun beaming through the trees.
She is a gentle fragrance in the breezy air.
She shines like a star.
She is a golden key opening to my glowing world.
She is like a pen that never stops working.
She is all the colours of the rainbow.
She is a dancing rose.
She is a yellow daffodil.
She is as wise as an owl.
She is a flower opening at the first sight of dawn.
She is the last beat left in my heart!

Georgina Cooper (10)
Wexham Court Primary School, Slough

She Is . . .

She is the rainbow on an overcast day
She is the boat on a turbulent ocean
She is the pillar holding up my world
She is the iced water on a sultry day
She is like a cup of happiness overflowing
She is the safety in my nightmare
She is like a ghostly white stallion cantering crazily with its free spirit
She is like the scent of a fresh new day
She is the beloved teddy clutched by a toddler
She is as unique as a single star in the whole of the vast night sky
Hidden in fine yellow sand, she is an ancient artefact, lurking
Undiscovered by the world.

Damayanti Chatterjee (10)
Wexham Court Primary School, Slough

Lent . . .

This year I'm giving up time
Time to keep my bedroom clean and tidy
Time to clear the kitchen sink and unclog the drain!
Time to sweep the living room
Time to help when I am ready
Time to do my bed sheet
Time to run down to the supermarket
Time to carry heavy dog houses
Time to help Mum when she is shattered
And sits down for a cup of coffee with biscuits
Time to give others care and respect
And in the end, time for all of you!

Tiggy Morten (10)
Wexham Court Primary School, Slough

She Is . . .

She is the soft, cosy duvet I snuggle up to at night.
She is the colours of the rainbow, gazing at me over the horizon.
She is a cosy cup of tea that I sip all the time.
She is as powerful as an eye of an eagle scanning me wherever I go.
She is the moat around my castle, guarding me all the time.
She is as beautiful as the purple rose in my golden garden.
She is as precious as Cleopatra's lost tomb.
She is like a fossil in my heart.
She is like the most expensive silk sari from the smallest village in China.

Luxana Rasiah (11)
Wexham Court Primary School, Slough

She Is . . .

She is a cosy blanket hugging me very tightly.
She is a flare of beautiful emotion.
She is a sunbeam through the blossom.
She is as precious as Tutankhamen's gold mask.
She is a star in my sky.
She is the biggest fossil in my heart.
She is as precious as Cleopatra's lost tomb.
She is the light of my life.
She is the Great Wall of China wrapping her arms around me.
She is my mum.

Abdul Mueez Raja (10)
Wexham Court Primary School, Slough

The Stone

The stone looks like a man's frozen heart,
It reminds me of an avalanche on Mount Everest,
It makes me feel like I'm being lulled to sleep in a cold, dark cave,
It sounds like a ghost's ghastly whisper,
It feels like I'm being hypnotised,
It tastes of bitter, dull acid rain,
It seems to mysteriously turn good into evil,
It can be used as a cat's frisbee,
It will make you do the opposite of your instinct,
The stone is evil - more evil than the wind's wicked whistle.

Wahab Mahmood (10)
Wexham Court Primary School, Slough

She Is . . .

She is as precious as the golden temple.
She is the Great Wall of China
Wrapping her arms around me.
She is my true inspiration.
She is as delicate as Cleopatra's lost tomb.
She is the golden ruby key that opens
The magical door to my life.
She is my one and only true hero.
She is like a heart-shaped fossil in me.

Shoaib Ahmed (10)
Wexham Court Primary School, Slough

She Is . . .

She is the magical crystal-white flower opening up its rare petals.
She is all the colours of the rainbow.
She is like a shiny star following a true path.
She is like a thick bandage wrapped around my heart.
She is like a strawberry sundae with exotic flavours.
She is like a firm rock which is unbreakable.
She is like Cleopatra's hidden treasure.
She is a genuine secret waiting to be revealed.

Sara Sarfraz (10)
Wexham Court Primary School, Slough

Mirror

The mirror is a twin reflection,
It reminds me of cold, solid ice.
It feels like smooth paper,
It sounds like old, rusty chimes.
It would taste like crispy chocolate,
It seems to make a weeping noise as soon as it cracks.
It can make a ghastly look as soon as I turn away.
It will haunt you for seven cold, dead years if you go near it.

Naadia Ajmal (10)
Wexham Court Primary School, Slough

The Earth

The genius brain spins in the darkness of space
Hypnotising inhabitants to love him
As a thousand names are on him, each like a brain cell
He has his own magic attracting everything that goes by.

Jaskirit Bhandal (10)
Wexham Court Primary School, Slough

Young Writers Information

We hope you have enjoyed reading this book - and that you will continue to enjoy it in the coming years.

If you like reading and writing poetry drop us a line, or give us a call, and we'll send you a free information pack.

Alternatively if you would like to order further copies of this book or any of our other titles, then please give us a call or log onto our website at www.youngwriters.co.uk.

Young Writers Information
Remus House
Coltsfoot Drive
Peterborough
PE2 9JX
(01733) 890066